TRAIL RIDES WITH TEQUILA:

A Journey of Faith

Marilyn Dexheimer Lawrence

TRAIL RIDES WITH TEQUILA: A Journey of Faith by
Marilyn Dexheimer Lawrence
Copyright © 2005, Marilyn Dexheimer Lawrence
ISBN # 0-89228-156-1

Impact Christian Books
332 Leffingwell Ave.,
Kirkwood, MO 63122
314-822-3309
www.impactchristianbooks.com

Cover Design: *Ideations*

TABLE OF CONTENTS

PREFACE

This book began as the story of a horse and rider who, over a period of years, became as one: in mind and body and spirit. In the process of writing, it also emerged as a record of a journey of faith. It took a leap of faith, in middle age, to pursue a childhood dream. It took faith to continue in the face of sometimes daunting challenges and setbacks. And it took enormous faith to continue when the dream, like all dreams, came to an end.

It was not an easy journey; few journeys are. But when we open our hearts to the love that is offered us, when we allow ourselves to be led in sometimes unexpected paths – when we follow our dreams – we are never alone. In my story, the dream of horses led me to the most special relationship of a lifetime, to a connection with one of God's creatures – and it led me to walk much more closely with the Creator Himself.

Pegasus is not just a myth. It is a dream for many of us. Horses truly give us wings; they lift us up and carry us farther and faster than we ever imagined. They open new worlds. For those who have been fortunate to realize their dreams – and for those who only dream – this book is for you. May it give you hope, and courage, and enjoyment – and may it renew your faith.

IN THE BEGINNING

*"Make me know thy ways, 0 Lord, teach me
thy paths."* Psalm 25

Like most little girls, I wanted a horse. I had
plenty of pets: cats, tropical fish, a cocker spaniel
named Terry who was my childhood companion and
best friend. But I wanted a HORSE. "We can't afford
a horse," my parents would say. "There is no place to
keep a horse." "You wouldn't take care of it." "You'd
get tired of it." "Who would feed it?" "What in the
world do you want a HORSE for?"

I was an active child, growing up in the small
town of Bedford, New York. My father, Charles
Frederick Dexheimer, was born in that town in the
year 1912. Twenty-two years later, a Methodist
minister came to town named Benjamin Denniston.
He had a beautiful daughter, Laura, who had just
graduated from finishing school. Laura and "Dex"
met, and married; I am a product of that union.

I am also the product of a small town in which I
was related to more people than I can count! Bedford,
located 40 miles north of New York City, was replete
with aunts, uncles, great-aunts and great-uncles,
grandparents, and cousins. I couldn't go anywhere

without running into a relative! But except for "crazy Aunt Jane" with her cats, none of them had pets.

I played every sport, explored the countryside on my bicycle, read voraciously and excelled in school. I grew up and went away to college, finished graduate school, got a job with a U.S. Senator in Washington. After six years on "the Hill," in which time I finished a doctoral dissertation, I moved to the Executive Office of the President as a Congressional Relations officer. I traveled the world and had an exciting life. But something kept drawing me to my childhood love: I wanted a HORSE!

The opportunity finally came in 1975. I accepted a position as Congressional Liaison Officer for the U.S. Information Agency. One day I happened to mention my lifelong dream to one of the Agency's senior officers (later Ambassador) Jock Shirley. Jock, it turned out, was an accomplished rider and polo player. He invited me to go with him to the Reston Polo Club, of which he was a member, and he saddled one of the quieter horses for me. We did a short trail ride. I was hooked!

I spoke with the instructor at the club, and signed up for weekly lessons. But there was an immediate problem: I lived in Washington, and I didn't own a car! A friend and former college classmate, Owen, had recently moved to Washington, and appealing to his sense of adventure, I persuaded him to take riding lessons with me. In retrospect, I cannot imagine why he agreed to it. Every Wednesday evening he had to drive in from Virginia where he worked, pick me up on Pennsylvania Avenue where I worked, and drive back out to Virginia – to do something that terrified him! He only lasted about six months, but the experience gave him a host of stories with which he still entertains his friends. It gave me a start in the direction that would totally change my life.

I did not ride Tequila at first. In fact, I did not even see Tequila at first. My mount in these weekly lessons was one or another of the school horses: an old gray, or an old chestnut, whose names are long since forgotten.

About two months into the program, in August during the Congressional recess, I was sent overseas for an "orientation trip" to some of our posts in Western and Eastern Europe. I was gone for a month: visiting London, Moscow, Leningrad, Belgrade, Vienna, Bonn, and assorted branch installations. Two days after I returned, Owen and I were back at the Polo Club for a Wednesday night lesson.

What I saw that night was far more memorable than anything I had seen in Europe. Even the gold of the Kremlin couldn't compare to the little golden horse. Our riding instructor, Judith Fiorentino, chose that night to take her beginning adult class on our first trail ride. I was riding one of the old school horses. The most experienced rider in the class was mounted on the newcomer. The horse pranced. He bucked. He tossed his head and flagged his tail. He threw his rider, twice. And as it grew dark and the moon fell full on his flaxen mane, I fell hopelessly in love.

For the next several weeks, when I arrived at the barn for my lessons, I hoped that I would be allowed to ride the newcomer. I learned that his name was Tequila. I brought him carrots. I spent extra time with him. And finally, one night in October, I was allowed to ride him – in a lesson, in the ring.

It was quite a switch from riding a horse I had to urge on with every step, to riding one that I had to try to hold back. That night we just did exercises at the walk and trot. But after a couple of lessons I was brave enough to start requesting Tequila when I came out with Owen or Jock for a Saturday morning trail ride.

Tequila was far more horse than I could handle. Every Friday night I would lie awake anticipating all the things that could go wrong: I could be thrown, I could be run away with, Tequila could step in a hole and get hurt, Tequila could step on ME! The possibilities were endless. I would arrive at the barn with an upset stomach and shaking hands. I would groom and saddle up, and we would be on our way. Even the trail rides, at first, were just walk-trot. If my riding companion wanted to canter or gallop, he would give me time to dismount and handgraze Tequila behind a hill or a stand of trees. Of course,

Tequila knew what was going on and he wasn't happy; he wanted to gallop, too. But most days we returned without mishap, and Tequila was rewarded with an hour or more of handgrazing before being put back in his stall.

In those days, Tequila was never turned out. When he first came to the Polo Club, he had been turned out with the other horses in the wide open fields that surrounded the barn. But within a few short weeks, the owners of the adjacent property became so irate that they threatened the Club with its first and only lawsuit. They had a lovely brick home with a wide green lawn and a white board fence around it. They also had a garden, where they delighted in raising their own vegetables. Tequila liked it, too. Several times a day he would pop over the white board fence and onto the wide green lawn, where he helped himself to the corn, the lettuce, the beet tops, and especially the carrots.

The manager of the Polo Club, Mike McCarrick, was also getting upset: he would frequently look out on an empty pasture, and discover that Tequila had taken off on some adventure and the rest of the horses had followed him. Calls started to come in about "loose horses" all up and down the roads.

There was no other solution but to confine Tequila to his stall, except when he was being ridden or when someone consented to handgraze him. At least that was the intent of the management. Tequila had other ideas. He was pretty; he was appealing; and frequently a visitor or another boarder would arrive at the barn and find him alone in his stall, looking longingly at the surrounding fields. Tequila was a con artist: he would nicker, he would step forward, big eyes and ears alert. If someone came close he would nuzzle or lick their hand. If the person looked, they would usually notice a stall totally devoid of hay or bedding. Tequila was omnivorous, and it was well known among the "regulars" that he once even ate the straw from a broom and left the handle lying in the muck.

Invariably, someone would take pity on him. If he were really lucky, they would assume he had been left in by mistake and they would turn him out. At the very least, they would find him a flake of hay or a handful of grain.

But Tequila wanted more. Soon the management would discover him gone – with his stall door locked behind him! At first no one could figure it out. Then one day a stable hand watched in amazement as Tequila, from a standstill, leaped over the Dutch door of his stall, made an immediate 90 degree turn down the aisle of the barn, and jumped the 5 foot fence that surrounded the barnyard.

Tequila escaped the day I bought him. I arrived at the barn that memorable Saturday morning to find what looked like a palomino unicorn. He had been out foraging on the woodline, and the brambles were so matted in his long forelock that it was standing straight up on end.

I didn't intend to buy Tequila. I didn't intend to buy a horse at all; I was just riding for fun. But one day after I had been riding him for about a month, I called the Club on a Thursday to "reserve" him for Saturday morning. "He may not be here," was Mike's response. One of the other adult riders had made an offer for him and was planning to move him to another farm.

Chris Appel-Bucierka was a much better rider than I, and she was just getting started on a career in vaulting. She felt that Tequila had the perfect build for a vaulting horse: smooth gaits, wide back, and not too far off the ground. She was right, as far as it went. But as my Dad used to say whenever my mother wanted to learn to drive, he "didn't have the temperament for it." I did not see Tequila as a vaulting horse at all. In fact, I realized with a start, I didn't see him as anyone's horse but MINE.

"How much did she offer? I'll pay you more," was my well-thought out response. He quoted a figure. I offered higher. He said, "Be here early Saturday morning with the money."

That Friday night and Saturday morning were even more anxiety-ridden than usual. Jock drove me out to the Club. We saddled our horses, I mounted Tequila, and we rode off into the woods – where we spent most of the day. Chris arrived to pick up "her" horse, and was told he wasn't there. He had been sold to someone else. There must have been some discussion, because it was mid-afternoon by the time we received word that it was safe to return to the barn. Tequila, of course, thoroughly enjoyed the outing: he had all that time out of his stall where he could be eating grass.

I should have felt guilty, and for a while I did. But Chris and I remained friends, and she went on to find a truly perfect vaulting horse – a stocky gray mare named Topaz, who, over the next twenty years, took Chris and her Topaz Vaulters to many national championships.

But in addition to the questionable ethics, I had done something else wrong. At the time, I didn't know that a horse was supposed to be "vetted" before he was purchased. I didn't know about physical infirmities and diseases, about annual shots and blood tests for transmittable diseases. Conformation – the angle of the shoulders and the legs, the set of the head and neck, the type of muscling in the rump – all meant nothing to me. I certainly didn't know anything about suiting a horse to a rider's interests and skill levels. My instructor, of course, did know such things, and the first thing she did when she learned what I had done was to call a veterinarian for a belated health check. He passed. But to my great shock and surprise, my new horse turned out to be not the seven-year old that the manager had estimated, but closer to 10 or 11 years of age.

By then, it didn't matter.

I paid $700 for the love of my life. I made an agreement with the Club that, in exchange for paying just half-board, they could continue to use Tequila in lessons. That suited their purposes: all the little girls loved him, and he was an exceptional jumper. And it worked well for me: I got a bit of a financial break – after all, I had never planned to own a horse. And Tequila got more of the exercise he needed, since at that point I was still coming out to the Club just twice a week.

Owning a horse, however, did mean additional responsibilities. First of all, Judith told me, I needed my own gear. The following week she took me to Dominion Saddlery in Chantilly, Virginia, where I made my first tack purchases.

It was my first trip to a saddlery, and the impressions will stay with me forever. There are people who are enamoured with tobacconists, rich in old world charms and heavy perfumes. There are those who like nothing better than the local hardware with its woods and metals and fertilizer smells. Others prefer the peculiar musty promise of old books. I am transported by the sights and smells of a saddlery: the row on row of shiny new saddles, the supple ranks of lead shanks and bridles, the rich warm leather smells garnished with the pungent scent of astringents. For me, a saddlery is a sensory treat.

I still have the sales slip from that day: I got a halter and leadline (in bright red; it came to be Tequila's color as it had always been mine); a tack box with brushes and curry comb and a hoofpick, and a leather bridle. A couple weeks later we went back and I added a saddle pad and my first saddle, a Keiffer Centaur.

With the purchase of a saddle, I was now a REAL horse owner. That day, when we returned to the club, Judith offered to take me on a trail ride. It was my first ride off the property, and we intended to celebrate my new status and my newfound joy.

It was a crisp, late fall day, and we saddled up and headed cross-country for Frying Pan Park in Herndon. Today the park is surrounded by housing developments and light industry. In those days, it was still clear sailing through woods and harvested cornfields.

We were doing well: an easy walk through the woods, a strong trot along the cornrows. We enjoyed the occasional scurry of a fox or a squirrel, the circling of a hawk overhead, the wonderful damp-sweet smell of fallen leaves. Frying Pan Park, then as now, is designed for cross-country competition, and it has a beautifully maintained open network of trails. It also has jumps, lots of them, and Tequila loved to jump. It was a skill that, as a beginning rider, I had not yet acquired.

We were trotting quietly along the trails, using

the detours around the jumps, when suddenly a thoughtless rider came cantering up behind us. Ignoring Judith's shouts to stop, he tried to pass us, heading for a 3-foot log jump that lay just ahead. Tequila was up to the challenge; I was not. He took off ahead of the rider, aimed straight for the jump, and apparently cleared it magnificently. I missed the sight. I was lying unconscious in front of the jump where I had struck my head on the logs as I fell!

The thoughtless rider, at that point, tried to "help." Again disobeying Judith, he went chasing after Tequila to catch him and bring him back. No horse has ever caught up with Tequila, and this day was no exception. When I came to, I learned that my new horse and all my new tack had disappeared into the woods.

Judith tried to get me to rest, but I would have none of it. I was too concerned about Tequila. Ignoring my throbbing head, I went out looking and calling, searching and hoping and listening. There was no sound. There was no whinny, no footfalls on the trail. All I could think of was finding him, having him safe: what if he got hurt out there? What if he tripped over his bridle, or got a stirrup leather caught on a branch? What if the saddle came lose and swung under his belly, and he hurt himself trying to run with it? What if someone stole him? What if I never saw him again?

We searched for hours, until it grew dark and my

instructor invited me to spend the night at her nearby house. It was another long and sleepless night, and at first light we were out searching again. We went from farmhouse to farmhouse, asking if anyone had seen a little horse wearing a saddle and bridle and wandering around loose. After a couple of hours we finished visiting most of the homes and farms in the area, and I was getting very discouraged indeed.

I walked up to one of the last farmhouses, where an old man sat on the porch enjoying his morning coffee. "Have you seen a little palomino horse wearing a saddle and bridle?" By now I was well past tears: I was getting desperate. "You mean that one?" He pointed. I spun around to see Tequila coming up the lane, heading for the barn, looking for his breakfast.

I raced to embrace him. He was trudging along as if in a trance, head down, clearly weary. He stopped, he nuzzled, he blew a sigh of relief. I took off his saddle and bridle, relieving the pressure on his back and at the corners of his mouth where the bit had rested for the last 18 hours. I put on his halter and leadline, and led him to a shady spot where he could eat some grass. The farmer's wife called the Polo Club, and someone located Judith. Within half an hour, she pulled up with the truck and horse trailer, and we loaded Tequila and drove him home. I don't know if HE was glad to be back, but I was certainly relieved. I brushed him, checked him thoroughly for cuts – there were none – fed him, and put him in his stall. Only then did I call my friend Owen to come out and get me and take me home.

The experience taught me a great deal – not just about safe riding practices, but about myself. I was surprised to learn how much I had come to care for another being – and in so short a time. After years of focusing on work, on achievement, on getting ahead in one of the most competitive environments in the world, I was shocked to discover that I LOVED this crazy creature, and was already putting him first. There was never a thought of returning to Washington – to work or other activities – until I was sure Tequila was safe. The concern with his well-being, the preference for his company, would cause rifts in some human relationships over the years, but I never regretted my choice or my commitment.

Soon it was Christmas, and I flew to California to spend the holidays with my family. Two years before, my parents had retired to their dream home, in Estes Park, Colorado. But my father had taken ill with a mysterious lung ailment, and the altitude proved too much for him. They had moved to Los Angeles where my younger sister lived and where he could get the medical attention that he needed.

I was in the habit of seeing my family once a year, and this time I was in for a shock. My Dad looked terrible! He couldn't walk a block without getting out of breath. He had lost weight. He hated being sick, and my mother and sister were afraid. It was a very strained vacation, with my parents living in a one-bedroom apartment a floor above my sister's, and with me sleeping on the couch and trying to understand all that was happening. Our family had never been very good at communicating, and words failed more than usual this Christmas. It was as if all the pain and the fear just further complicated our discourse: we simply couldn't talk to each other.

I was relieved to return to Washington, and my family knew it. It would take me another 20 years to develop the faith, and the sensitivity, and the communications skills that could have bridged the barriers. Instead, this time, I put the pain behind me and got on with my own life. Tequila became a refuge and a comfort. More and more, I looked forward to my weekly lessons and to the weekend trail rides. I began renting a car on Saturday mornings and keeping it til Sunday night; that way I could spend both days with my horse. My social life, seldom a major factor in my life, purely and simply TANKED.

In late January I made a trip to Africa to attend a conference for the U.S. Information Agency. While overnighting in Madrid on the way home, I received a call from the Agency's General Counsel: my father was in the hospital, and his condition was serious. By the time I got back to Washington, however, he had stabilized. He was moved to a nursing home where, my mother assured me, he could remain for several months.

I had barely begun to get back into the routine of riding and preparing for Congressional hearings when I was awakened at 4 o'clock one morning by a phone call from my mother in Los Angeles. My father had passed away a few hours before. The funeral would be in three days, in their old church in Houston, Texas. I scrambled to get a flight, arriving the day before the service, and remembering almost nothing of the days that followed. My father had been a "traveling sales manager," a distant but honored figure in my childhood; but in my adult years we had achieved a real friendship. We wrote each other faithfully every week, and our letters went on for pages at a time debating the major issues of the day. We enjoyed each other. And now he was gone.

Returning to Washington, and thinking about what had happened, I came to a clear realization. While I knew my Dad was ill, I had not realized HOW ill, and his death came as a shock. I regretted that I had not made another trip to California; that I had not been there for him, to talk with him, as he faced the greatest passage of all. Tequila was now the most loved, the most important being in my life, and I was determined not to make the same mistake with him. If anything happened to him, if he ever needed me, I wanted to BE there, immediately. That, I reasoned, required that I own a car.

This time I discussed the problem with Judith, and she, as usual, came up with a solution. She and her husband were planning to sell their old Mercury Cougar and buy a much more practical station wagon. Would I like to have the Cougar? I jumped at the opportunity, and soon was the proud owner of my very first automobile: a dark green hard top with tan leather bucket seats and the classic lines that only the 1969 edition ever seemed to achieve. "Cougar" became my means of reaching Tequila, and I put that car to a lot of use.

The lessons continued. The trail rides became more frequent. Though Owen had dropped out of the riding program, there were other beginning adults in the class, who soon adjusted to the fact that Judith had to SPELL her instructions! Tequila had quite a vocabulary, and if he heard the command "canter" or "trot" or "walk," he responded immediately. It had taken Judith a while to realize that it was Tequila who was obeying her instructions – I was just along for the ride.

But even with my increased schedule and with his continued use in lessons, Tequila wasn't getting enough exercise. There was also another problem which, with my inexperience, I was slow to realize. The Club was going downhill. Development was encroaching; it was the mid-1970s and Fairfax County was undergoing a major construction boom. Crossroads were becoming new communities almost overnight; bucolic farmlands were being transformed into developments; tree-lined trails were being paved over. Some of the better riders were moving farther out, and with the loss of revenue, the care of the horses was declining. It was getting harder to get good barn help at a reasonable wage. The manager was forced to begin cutting back on feed. Judith, who kept her own horses at the Club, began buying her own supply of hay and grain which she graciously shared with Tequila.

Then came heavy spring rains, and the barns not only leaked, the stalls actually flooded. Tequila, who stood in his stall all day, was one of the first to feel its effects: he began to develop thrush, a bacterial infection in the soles of his feet, which required constant medication and packing with cotton.

It was during this time that Tequila started to undergo an "attitude change." He hated being confined most of the day. He wasn't getting enough food. His stall was wet, and the new hired help were not as efficient or as caring. He took a strong dislike to certain of the stablehands, refusing to let them into his stall: he would back into a corner, arch his neck, snort and if that didn't work, wheel and threaten to kick.

One awful day, a visiting instructor arrived to give a jumping clinic at the Club. Jerry Castelman, at that time, held the world's indoor high jump record on a horse; he was a star. Several people had arrived for the clinic, not just from our club but from surrounding barns. Many of them were excellent riders, and they had worked out a synchronized pattern at one end of the ring: they would trot or canter in sequence over a jump or series of jumps, with the instructor shouting out instructions or offering critiques. All was going smoothly.

I was riding Tequila at the other end of the huge ring, practicing simple walk-trot-canter exercises. But Tequila loved to jump, and he suddenly decided that what was going on at the other end of the ring looked a lot more interesting. Without warning – which was the way he did everything – he suddenly broke into a gallop and charged into the middle of the class. Riders scattered in all directions; collisions were narrowly averted. Even I – beginner that I was – realized that serious injuries could have resulted from his little prank. Jerry realized something else – that I had no control over my mount. His words were succinct and to the point, and I will hear them as long as I live: "If you value your life, you'll get off that horse and never get on him again."

THE EXODUS

"I have come to bring them to a land flowing with milk and honey."

Exodus 3:8

I was crushed. I dismounted and led Tequila back to the barn, untacked him, and handgrazed him for hours. I learned later, there had been much discussion among the "professionals" at the barn about Tequila and me. Jerry's views were strongly reinforced by an experienced rider in his clinic, Francesca, who later became his wife. Some months before, Francesca had taken Tequila out with the Fairfax Hunt. She returned swearing never to ride him again: he had raced, and apparently beaten, every horse in the field – including the Master's. Francesca's shoulders and arms had ached for a week from the futile effort to hold him back. No one knew how a beginning rider would ever be able to handle him.

I looked at my lifelong dream, at the horse I now loved. Would I have to give him up? NO!! Though I couldn't have defined it at the time, I was being led by faith; Tequila had come into my life for a reason. All I knew then was that I would not give him up; rather, I would try to become as good a rider as he was a horse. The journey would begin with assuming full responsibility, both for his well-being and my own. There would be no more sharing him with other riders, and I would HAVE to get him to another boarding stable where he would have better care. His feet were becoming more infected despite our ministrations, and his attitude was deteriorating. For probably the only time in his life, he was not a happy horse.

It was not just a matter of finding a stable close enough to the city to be accessible for me. The stable had to be able to accommodate HIM: a fence-jumping, stall-jumping, independent horse who required a great deal of special handling. It had to have clean, dry, roomy stalls with floor to ceiling walls and doors. It had to have access to trails. And it had to permit a visiting instructor; I wanted to continue my lessons with Judith.

I must have looked at 20 boarding facilities and barns in Northern Virginia before I found Stoneridge Farm, in Great Falls. I had not looked there at first because it was a show barn and Judith didn't think we would be happy there. She was wrong!! Stoneridge had everything I wanted. There was a large, professional main barn, originally built to house the Marriott racing stable. There were two large outdoor rings with a new indoor ring in the offing. The stalls were roomy, with full length walls and doors, and heavy wire grating above the wall on the aisle side. Having my own instructor would not be a problem, and I could make my own turnout arrangements. I only had to wait for a vacancy.

Finally, in September 1976, ten months after I bought Tequila, a stall came available. I took the day off from work – it was a Wednesday – and Judith and I loaded Tequila onto her trailer and vanned him the six miles to Stoneridge. It was to be his home, and mine, for the next 13 years.

We got Tequila settled in a clean dry stall, gave him hay and water, and I returned to Washington to work, confident that he would be safe and secure until I returned on Saturday morning. I left specific instructions that he was not to be turned out, either with other horses or alone; I would take care of his exercise myself

The owner of Stoneridge thought it was cruel to keep Tequila penned up for the better part of four days. She looked at this little horse with her experienced eye and thought I must be mistaken; there was no way he would jump a fence. And so the next day she turned him out.

She used caution. She put him in an enclosure known as "the run." It was nothing more than a fenced-off portion of a dirt road, with six-foot high board and American wire fencing, and metal cattle gates on each end. The fence on the side toward the barn was built on top of an embankment and covered with honeysuckle. The fence on the far side sat lower down the embankment with a drop-off into the woods on the neighboring farm. No horse, before or after, had ever escaped from it.

As I heard the story later, Tequila stayed in "the run" for less than five minutes. He was over the fence on the far side, into the woods, and GONE. He loved every minute of his escapade, and he made the most of it. He ran loose for hours while the barn owner and all the employees tried to catch him with ropes, sweet feed, hay, and any other enticement they could imagine. Finally he surrendered – at suppertime.

He was none the worse for wear when I arrived on Saturday morning for our customary turnout and trail ride. In fact, he was feeling quite proud of himself. As was my custom, I first exercised him in the ring, allowing him to walk, trot and canter in both directions on a long line to warm him up and to get the "kinks" out. Then I saddled and mounted up. We rode up the dirt lane, through some woods, and into a little clearing. It was a crisp fall day, and Tequila wanted to run. He started to jig, and then to buck. I was alone, and afraid. For the first time I had my horse out in territory I didn't know, with no one around whom I knew or could ask for help. There was only one place to turn. I dismounted, and started talking to Tequila.

It was our first really serious conversation, as I stood beside him, and looked him straight in the eye. I told him this new barn was much better than the one we had left. I told him he would have a clean dry stall, and plenty of food, in the new place. I told him that I loved him and wanted to be his friend, but that he would have to work with me. I had a lot to learn, and I asked for his patience. In return, I would be patient with him. We were together now, and we had to work this out.

I don't believe he understood a single word I said. But I DO believe that he understood what I meant. For the first time, a human was treating him as an equal, not as someone who wanted to dominate or control. He looked at me with great interest. We stood there for several minutes, communicating, sometimes with words, sometimes with gestures and thoughts.

When I remounted, I could sense a difference. He was quieter, more trusting, more giving. And I began to trust him. We enjoyed the rest of the trail ride, came back to the barn, and I handgrazed him for a long time. I do not say that there were no more difficulties – there were plenty. But Tequila and I, in less than a year, had made the transition from horse and owner to the beginning of a true partnership.

I started changing my pattern after that. Instead of coming out one night a week for lessons, I started coming out twice a week, early in the mornings, for grooming and turnout and trail rides. I worked out an arrangement with my office so that, at least on days when there were no hearings or meetings, I could come in to work at 10 or 10:30 a.m. and stay until 7 or 8 p.m. In actual fact, the new schedule worked better for everyone. Most Congressional offices do not get going until about 10 a.m., and then they work late into the evenings. It turned into a net plus – for the Agency, our Congressional committees, for me – and for Tequila.

Gradually, Tequila was becoming a happier horse. He still didn't trust veterinarians or blacksmiths or barn help. But he had a big, clean stall; he was being fed better; he was being ridden by only one person; and he was coming to trust me. He was getting into a regular routine, and he liked it.

At first I spent hours handgrazing him in the field. Then gradually, as he became more settled and more familiar with his surroundings, I began turning him loose in the front field. I stayed with him, but he adapted well and thoroughly enjoyed the freedom.

The horse in the stall next to him, a chestnut thoroughbred mare named Sugar, was becoming a friend. Her owners would sometimes bring her down to the front field, too, and the horses would graze together. Tequila and Sugar were on the way to becoming companions; they shared adjoining stalls for thirteen years. And Sugar's owners, Jean and George Schaeffer, were becoming friends of mine as well. The Schaeffers and I shared a love of art, and music, and travel. We would sit and talk for hours, or turn on the car radio and listen to classical music, while our horses grazed. Jean was a University of Chicago graduate who had worked in the travel industry before meeting George; they married in

Mexico City. George was a graduate of Holy Cross who worked for the CIA. Among the three of us, we not only cared for our own horses, but came to look after our friends' horses as well, and fed all the barn cats for good measure.

Then, just as things were going well, Tequila suffered his first injury. It was late November, and one day on the trail he came up lame. I rested him a couple days, but the lameness persisted, and there was heat in his right front leg. The barn veterinarian looked at it and said it was probably a stone bruise. I was not satisfied with the diagnosis and called the veterinarian I had used before.

That action precipitated a minor diplomatic crisis: the barn veterinarian was under contract to care of all the horses at the barn. But I wanted "Dr. Dave" Hall, who had treated Tequila at the Polo Club and who, coincidentally, had helped build Stoneridge back when it belonged to the Marriott family. He came out the next day, and diagnosed a pulled suspensory ligament, which necessitated several weeks of rest and handgrazing. But at least I knew what was wrong and how to treat it.

"He's one of the most difficult horses I've ever had to work with," Dr. Dave told me, "not because of any bad habits, but simply because he's afraid of me. He's what I call a 'one person horse'." This particular day, it took Dave half an hour just to lift Tequila's right front foot. But, he said with satisfaction, "I finally got his confidence."

Making decisions regarding Tequila's care was a critical part of becoming a true partner with him. It also proved essential, especially in the years to come, that I developed the knack of making independent judgments about who would care for him and what professional advice I would follow. Over the years, Tequila would prove to be challenging in more ways than one, and one of those ways would definitely be medical.

I had moved Tequila to Stoneridge in September, 1976; three months later, my mother and sister came for Christmas. It was the first Christmas after my father had died, and a bittersweet time for us all. I had much to show them: a new apartment at Columbia Plaza in Washington D.C.; a new car – and most of all, my new horse. They liked the car and the apartment, but they never reconciled themselves to the horse.

My mother and sister gamely came to the barn. Tequila had recovered to the point that I could at least mount him and ride him at a walk. I just had to show him off.

They watched me ride – from a safe distance outside the fence. But they were clearly frightened by the whole experience of being around horses, and of seeing me riding one. They didn't like the smells of the barn: the dust, the hay, the sweet odor of grain, and particularly the odor of horses. Mother couldn't wait to get back in the car where she felt safe and clean.

Just before I put Tequila back in his stall I led him over to the car so Mother could say "good bye" to him. Mother had just had her hair done, and it smelled sweet to him. He stretched his nose in the car window and began nuzzling her hairdo to see if there was a treat lodged in it somewhere. In her outrage at the assault, Mother promptly went from being skeptical to having an absolute antipathy to this newest member of the "family." She never changed.

All healthy animals are curious about their environment, and watching them explore, poke, test, nuzzle, try to identify and relate, is one of the great and endless joys of being with them.

Tequila was more curious than most. I have watched hundreds of horses standing in the aisle of a barn or in their stalls. Some will stand still for hours. Some will go to sleep. Most will eat food if it is put in front of them. A few object to being tied in the aisle and will try to break their ties and bolt.

But I have never seen a horse go through the range of antics of Tequila. If he was tied in the aisle, even for a few minutes, he would first paw and nuzzle all over the floor looking for food, or try to eat bits of grain or hay embedded in the cracks of the wall. He would watch everyone and everything that moved, sometimes reacting in fear of a person or a stick;

sometimes displaying extraordinary friendship and interest if it appeared they might be carrying food. He would greet every horse that went by, nuzzle every barn cat that passed underfoot.

Leading him around the barn, it was clear that no bag, pail, cloth, mechanical implement, person, automobile or fencepost was free from his inquiring muzzle. Every bag had to be lifted in his teeth and shaken out in search of a stray pellet. Every pail had to be inspected inside and out, knocked over to make sure there was nothing edible underneath. The incident with my mother in the car was far from unique. Tequila was known for plunging his nose into open trucks and cars where, with minimal effort and exploration, he usually emerged triumphantly with a bag of carrots, an apple, cookies or potato chips – even a bale of hay.

Tequila was fascinated by his own shadow. I think I was as intrigued as he, one day as we walked up the lane toward the barn with the sun at our backs, and I realized that he had his nose to the ground exploring the dimensions of the shadow that preceded him. Nor was it just his shadow that interested him. He loved to look at his reflection in a glass. One side of the barn had a large window with one-way glass, and it was often hard to get Tequila past the sight of his own image that miraculously appeared to him on the side of the wall. There was an indoor riding ring at a neighboring facility that had large metal reflectors along the wall. Their purpose was to enable riders to see what they were doing as they rode along; in our case the situation was reversed, and it was Tequila who studied his image in passing.

Snow also captured his attention, and ice. At the first annual appearance of either, he would step outside the barn, paw at the strange new substance, sniff at it, even taste it. If it was ice, he would proceed gingerly across the patch til he found more stable footing. If he came to a frozen stream, he would sniff and snort, and break the ice with his hoof before proceeding across. If there was fresh snow, he would relish the chance to buck, roll, and carry on like the carefree foal he always remained in his heart.

He was equally curious with people. While he maintained a lifelong aversion to most men, he was keenly aware that he could charm women and children. He would forever reach out, to nuzzle, greet, beg – he was a shameless beggar – and more often than not, his efforts were rewarded. "He's so cute," they would say as they gave him a carrot or a treat. He quickly became a barn favorite – and just as quickly began to put on weight. After a few months, I had to post a sign on his stall saying: "Please do not feed me. My Mommy says I am overweight and it is not good for me." It helped a little, but not very much.

Tequila had another habit that some of the boarders at the barn never caught on to. They would tie their horses in front of Tequila's stall to groom them or prepare them for a show – and find to their amazement that their equipment was disappearing. They would search the barn, blame other boarders, think they were becoming forgetful. It never occurred to some of them that the culprit might be facing them on the other side of the wire, looking at them through a long blond forelock with innocent brown eyes.

Tequila had, in fact, dug a hole underneath the wall of his stall, and to stave off boredom he would stick his nose and his tongue through the aperture and pull anything he could find into his stall. Sometimes he got lucky and found food – a flake of hay someone had set down to put into a haynet for the trip, a bag of carrots they were planning to feed their own horse, even some spilled grain. Most times, though, what he found was just something to play with. It was not at all unusual for me to arrive at the barn in the evening after work and find, buried in his bedding, brushes, combs, leadlines, articles of clothing. One time I caught him in the act of burying not just one but TWO very expensive show bridles that someone had made the grave mistake of hanging within his reach.

My friend Owen had long since given up riding, though he carried his chaps and his goofy white hardhat around in the trunk of his car for another 20 years, and frequently bragged about how he had taken riding lessons. He would occasionally come to the barn to watch, and one day he stood with Judith in amazement as I trotted a half-circle around them and took off up the hill and across the field – at a full gallop. He had seen Tequila and me gallop before, but this was the first time he had seen us do it intentionally. Judith turned to him and said, "What do you see?" He replied, "She looks like she's part of that horse." Tequila and I were on the way to becoming one.

Judith believed firmly that every rider should have the experience of competing in a horse show. So one day, after I had been taking lessons from her for a year and a half, and was happily ensconced at Stoneridge Farm, Judith announced that she was picking me up on Saturday morning and taking me to a show, at the old Polo Club grounds. "It's just a local show," she said, "and it will be good experience for you."

I wasn't sure I wanted to go back to the Polo Club, and I was not at all sure how Tequila would react to the experience. But I did all the hours of necessary preparation: polished my boots, polished Tequila's feet, shampooed my horse and put whiting in his mane and tail (I refused to pull his mane short and braid it as she wanted me to do.) I diligently cleaned my saddle and bridle, laundered my saddle pad, brushed my jacket; and on the appointed day we were ready to go.

Tequila knew instantly where he was: he would never forget that barn, that ring, those fields. He came off the trailer and headed straight for the lower barn, where he had lived. With me walking beside him holding his leadline, he went directly to the last stall on the left: it had been his stall. He stood looking at it, and I swear to this day, he shook his head and shuddered!

We entered several "flat classes": basic walk, trot and canter competitions. After the first class, Judith said, "OK, what did you do wrong?" I didn't know. Apparently, at some point, Tequila had picked up the wrong lead (the leading front foot) at the canter, and that put us "out of the ribbons." I was too befuddled to notice, and I certainly wasn't going to admit to her that I still didn't know how to ask for the correct lead, that I always let Tequila do what he felt was right.

We did win one ribbon that day – my first and only one. We were in a class with several larger horses, and Tequila sped right past them as we picked up the canter. "Oho, we've blown it again" was my instant thought. But I let him go at his pace, more concerned with his comfort than with winning. To my great surprise, that is what earned us third place. "You didn't try to check him," the judge said, "You let him go at the pace that was comfortable for him, and that was the right thing to do." I learned a valuable lesson that day.

A couple of years later, Tequila and I entered another show, this one at a riding center near the Potomac River in Great Falls. It was a big show: hundreds of horses and riders, dozens of trailers and vans. I had decided on the spur of the moment to give showing another try, and we had hitched a ride on the Stoneridge van. We were neat and clean, and I have several photos taken by a friend that show a handsome horse and rider combination as we circled the course. This time Tequila was sure he had won, and when they called other horses instead, my wonderful mount stepped forward on his own.

There were several comments from people who had known Tequila at the Polo Club: they could not get over how good he looked, how well behaved he was, how much he seemed to have calmed down. Actually, Tequila was bored. We entered three or four classes, mutually decided we were not having any fun – and simply left the show grounds and hacked the six miles back to our own barn.

I will never forget the joy we both felt, after a long hot ride, when we entered our own back field. No other horses were turned out there at the time, and I shut the gate, removed Tequila's saddle and bridle and propped them against a tree. Then I took off my own jacket and boots – and BOTH of us enjoyed a delicious roll in the grass. By mutual consent, we never showed again.

Our lessons continued for a while longer, until Judith moved to Alabama. But they were becoming less a source of pleasure, for both Tequila and me. There was one terrible lesson in July of 1977. The temperature hovered around 100 degrees. Judith was in a hurry to finish the lesson and get on the road to

Pennsylvania where she was looking at a horse that was for sale. It was high noon and Tequila, who was smarter than either of us, did NOT want to engage in a jumping lesson.

Without any preliminaries, Judith said, "OK, canter toward that coop and let's see how you do." We cantered toward the coop – but we didn't clear it. Tequila swerved at the last split second, dropped his right shoulder, and deposited me on the ground. Unfortunately the first thing to hit the ground was my right arm, which promptly broke in two places, along with shattering my right wrist. It was the first broken bone I'd ever had, but it was a spectacular break!

Judith retrieved Tequila and my friend George untacked him and put him in his stall. Judith took me to the nearest emergency clinic, where we sat for an hour until someone determined that I really needed more help than they could provide. They gave me an ice pack, and we set off for the emergency room of Inova Fairfax Hospital, 45 minutes away.

At this point Judith had given up all hope of getting to Pennsylvania. We got to Fairfax Hospital, and waited. And waited. "Why can't somebody just put a cast on this thing and let me out of here?" I demanded impatiently. Finally a doctor appeared: Pat Palumbo, orthopedic surgeon extraordinaire, former team physician for the Washington Redskins. "I was in the library researching this break," was his opening line. I started to get the idea that this was not going to be a simple process. "It's a Smith's fracture," was his explanation. "I usually have to do surgery or put these in traction." He was willing to take a chance on simply resetting and casting it, but the process came with detailed instructions as to what I was NOT to do for the next few weeks. When the cast was finished, it reached to my shoulder, and my arm was bent upward at the elbow, a position I held for the next four weeks.

It was late afternoon by the time we were finished, and Judith and I headed back to the barn. Tequila was standing in his stall, sweating heavily – not from the heat, which was still oppressive, but from anxiety about his "Mom." I brushed him with my good hand, patted him, and gave him his carrots. And then it was time to go back to my apartment in Washington. Judith drove me home while another friend drove my car. I walked in the door with my cast and my pain-killers, and realized I was STUCK THERE.

At first I was in so much pain it didn't matter. But I quickly began to realize the limitations I faced: I couldn't dress myself. I couldn't wear my own clothes, because almost everything had sleeves. I couldn't drive. And I certainly could not ride. After one day of invalidism, I walked to the nearest clothing store, bought some sleeveless tops, and went back to work.

We had a "mark up" of the Agency's authorization

bill that week, and I showed up in slacks and a sleeveless striped top, with my arm in that horrible cast. The budget officer for the Agency later estimated that I earned several million dollars for us with that appearance – the Congressmen voted for increases out of sympathy. I knew it wasn't my powers of persuasion that had had an impact: I was in too much pain, and too "gooned" on medication, to be of any practical use.

Once again, I was dependent on others to get to the barn to see Tequila. Two or three times a week I would find someone willing to drive me out, and I would spend time grooming and handgrazing him, or watching him in the field. Of course my non-riding friends thought I was absolutely out of my mind. But anyone who had a horse and rode understood fully: breaks like this just go with the territory. "If you can't afford to fall, you shouldn't be riding" was a phrase that stayed with me throughout my career. My friends Jean and George, who came to the barn every day, turned Tequila out for me with their mare, Sugar. But it was a difficult few weeks for both of us.

It was during this time that Judith decided to teach Tequila, and me, the proper way to approach a fence. One day she came to the barn to give Tequila a proper lesson. She chose to do it in the front field, where several people gathered to watch. Judith was almost six feet tall, and looked like a giant on my little horse. She was a strong and decisive rider, experienced, a member of the Fairfax Hunt and a keen three-day event competitor. I stood with my cast propped up on a fence rail, watching with interest.

She started out trotting in small circles, explaining her leg and hand positions as she went along. Finally it came time to approach the fence, and in a loud, clear voice she said as she rode toward the obstacle, "Now you don't want him running out to the right, so you keep your <u>right</u> leg on him, and you keep a strong hold on the <u>left</u> rein and don't let him get his head around...."

Tequila cantered toward the fence, listening carefully, and at the last second before he would have taken off on the jump, he spun to the LEFT, dropped his LEFT shoulder, and deposited Judith on the ground. She came to her feet cursing "little horses that can turn on a dime." The little culprit, meanwhile, came trotting over to where I stood watching in my wrist-to-shoulder cast. His head was high, his neck was arched, his tail was standing erect, and he was proud as punch. He stopped in front of me and his eyes said, plain as day, "Didn't I do good, Mom?"

I did the only thing I could do. I laughed, I hugged him, and I said "Good Boy." To her eternal credit, Judith remained my friend. But I often wished that she could have seen him one night a few months later. He was turned out to graze in that same field while, at the other end of the field, the owner of the barn was teaching a children's jumping class. Tequila kept glancing at the youngsters and their ponies, and I could see the excitement building. Whether he wanted to teach them a lesson himself, or whether he just wanted to jump, I would never know. But suddenly his head came up, his ears perked, and he trotted into the middle of the class, where he proceeded to jump the entire course of fences, on his own.

After four weeks the break began to stabilize, and Dr. Palumbo thought it safe to cut the cast in half; at that point it only went to my elbow. I began riding again. Of course, it took three people to get me up into the saddle, because my right arm was still totally useless. I had to ride using a technique called "neck-reining," which can be done with one hand. The rider simply lays the reins against one side of the horse's neck or the other to indicate direction. He cooperated beautifully. It was a joy, for both Tequila and me, to at least walk and trot in the paddocks. And I could drive my car again. It was a quick recovery, and to the surprise even of my doctor, I regained full mobility. Soon, we were back to our regular schedule, exploring the countryside together.

Then came the winter of 1978. In January a blizzard blew in, and the Washington area was under three feet of snow. Government offices were closed, but the "holiday" did me no good. I couldn't get to the barn anyway because of the ice and snow that made the roads impassable. Once more I was dependent upon my friends to get Tequila out of his stall for exercise, to give him treats, to care for him. I didn't like it, and neither did he. It was almost a week before I was able to see him again, and during that week I started thinking about making other arrangements, this time, for myself. Maybe the "Exodus" would not be complete until we were both in the Promised Land.

I weighed the decision carefully. I had always hated commuting, and the thought of living anywhere that I couldn't walk to work was anathema to me. The spring and summer went along smoothly enough: I was able to get to the barn during the week and to spend long weekends there. Maybe this arrangement would work well after all, I began to reason.

Then in October of 1978, Tequila had an unfortunate reaction to a routine procedure administered by the barn veterinarian: fall shots and worming. He developed a stiff neck, he became lethargic, he lost interest in eating, his steps were shuffling. This continued for an entire weekend; two other horses at the barn showed the same symptoms.

Once more I called "Dr. Dave" and described the situation to him. "Mix six tablespoons of baking soda into some pellets and feed it to him," he said. "I think it's abdominal cramping and spasms." The owner of the barn thought I was crazy: what horse would eat baking soda? Tequila ate it. He perked up. I hopped on him bareback and rode in the field for a few minutes. He showed relief – both physically and psychologically – and by the next day he was fine.

I was relieved and so was he. But I also started

thinking again: what if the symptoms had occurred on a weekday? What if I hadn't been there to take care of him? Could he have developed severe stomach cramps and colicked? Could the stress and an elevated temperature have produced a frequently fatal hoof condition called founder?

Horses, for all their size and strength, are very fragile animals. A condition such as colic or founder is comparable to a heart attack or stroke in a human, in the sense that it can come on suddenly, it can be fatal, and it has the best prognosis if treated promptly. Once more I began to think seriously about moving to Great Falls myself.

A few months later, Tequila did colic. This time, also, it was in response to a routine worming, and fortunately, once again, the problem developed on a weekend. For one whole night, Tequila was miserable. His stomach cramped, he went down, he tried to roll, he couldn't eat. I stayed beside him, walking him to relieve the crippling gas pains and also to keep him from rolling. The owner of the barn gave him shots of Banamine to relax the muscles in his stomach.

Colic is not only an extremely painful condition, it can lead to ruptured or twisted intestines if the horse is allowed to roll. Such moments were not exactly what I had dreamed of when I wanted a horse of my own! But just as I had during that awful time at Frying Pan Park when Tequila was gone overnight, I totally focused on getting him safe and well.

It was a very cold night, and most of the boarders had gone home. As Tequila began tentatively to munch on some hay in his stall about 11 p.m., I saw car lights coming up the drive. It was a wonderful, thoughtful friend, bringing me some dinner. And it was not just any dinner. Mary had packed an elaborate picnic basket: there was roast chicken, mashed potatoes with gravy, salad, vegetables, hot tea and dessert. She even brought china and silver, which we set up on a tack trunk in the middle of the aisle. We had everything but candles – which we couldn't have used in the barn anyway.

Refreshed, and reassured that my horse was feeling better, I went into his stall and stood talking to him. Finally, feeling exhausted from the tension and the late hour, and suffering chills in the 20 degree barn, I sat down in the shavings. Tequila promptly lay down next to me and put his head in my lap. We rested that way until sometime in the early morning, both thankful, for health, for each other, and for wonderful friends.

The decision to move was made that night, and in the spring I made the plunge. One lovely Saturday when the hillsides were greening and the redbuds were coming into bloom, I walked into a real estate office in Great Falls Center and said, "What do you have available that is within walking distance of Stoneridge Farm?" The realtor showed me several photos, discussed a few options, we settled on a reasonable price range, and he took me for a drive.

After passing a couple of places that were either too expensive or too far away, we drove past a small split-foyer about a mile and a half from the barn. It was in a new development – the roads weren't even cut through yet, though eventually there would be one that came out on the main road right across from the stable. The house had been occupied by renters for six months and was already in disrepair: they were two truck drivers who occasionally parked their gargantuan rigs right on the lawn.

"I'll take it." I said. The realtor was aghast. "Don't you even want to see the inside?" he asked in amazement. He showed me through the interior, I pronounced it acceptable, and we went back and drew up an offer. Two months later, the house was mine. My good friend Owen came out and repainted the inside for me before I moved in; I got the carpets cleaned; I bought a lawnmower and a ladder; and I moved in. For the next nine years, until I retired from the Federal Government and Tequila and I moved to our own farm near Warrenton, it would be my home.

Owen, always the good friend, helped me move. Together we arranged the furniture and hung the pictures. Some friends from the barn arrived with a dogwood tree as a house-warming present. I cooked a spaghetti dinner and we shared a bottle of wine. That night, after everyone left, I slept for the first time in my own house. The Exodus was complete; I had made it to the Promised Land.

SONG OF SONGS

"He maketh me to lie down in green pastures;
he restoreth my soul." Psalm 23

The grass was rich and green that spring, and Tequila and I both enjoyed having more time together. One day shortly after I moved, I turned him out and watched: after a few preliminary bucks and a good roll, he settled down to eat. The sun was getting warm, and for a long time he ignored the two big bays – a gelding and a mare – who were turned out in the field with him. They wanted to play, and they finally got his attention. I watched with glee. Tequila's head came up, his ears perked, his tail went up like a flag. There was a deep snort, and he was off! He led the bays by eight lengths, from one end of the field to the other. It was a third of a mile, at a full gallop, with a pause for prancing and regrouping at each end. Back and forth they raced. It was a glorious sight: the two 16-hand bays and the 14:3-hand palomino who was always in the lead, galloping joyously up and down the field.

When they finally stopped at the gate, the bays were soaking wet and breathing hard. Tequila was literally trotting circles around them, still ready to play, neck arched, tail in the air. When it was clear that the game was over, he came trotting up to me. He nuzzled, and his expression said, "Did I show them, Mom?" He sure did. And he showed me, too, yet another reason why I so loved and enjoyed him.

Our lives changed considerably after I moved to Great Falls. I hadn't been in my new house a week when I had my first houseguest: a college classmate arrived from Seattle to attend a conference in Washington, and he came out to my new house for dinner. "Aren't we going to go by the barn to see Tequila?" he asked. "No," I answered. "I've had a rough day at work, and all I want to do is have a glass of wine and fix dinner. Just because I live out here doesn't mean I'm going to see Tequila every day."

How little I knew myself! Within the week, I was jumping off the commuter bus, running for my car, and eagerly driving the two miles to the barn to see my horse – every night! The commute actually gave me the first regular schedule I ever had. Because I was tied to a bus schedule, and because the bus only ran twice a day, I had no choice but to leave work on time every day. It didn't take long to discover how much I liked it.

Work in Washington had always been demanding, and there were times during Congressional hearings or tight budget fights on the Hill when long and dedicated hours were essential. But when I had lived in Washington, I often found myself staying late at the office, or coming in on weekends, when it wasn't really necessary. I would wait around at night for an "important" phone call from the Hill, or come in on a Saturday morning to check the cable traffic from an overseas problem area.

Partly, I must admit, I was doing it for the company. There was always someone else working late or on the weekend, too, and a half-hour chat with a colleague, which sometimes turned into lunch or dinner, sure beat sitting home alone.

When I got Tequila, that started to change: I no longer came in on weekends. But the move to Great Falls changed it even more, and improved the quality of my life enormously. For the first time since childhood, I was getting out and playing every day! I saw sunrises and sunsets – often from the back of my horse. I ran in the rain, and hiked through the snow, and most importantly, I felt a growing oneness with nature and with God's creation.

Life in the city had separated me from the natural flow of life. I lost the sense of being part of something greater than myself. I lost an awareness of harmony, and the sense of wonder that comes from viewing a star-studded sky, or the first spring violet, or a great buck silhouetted on top of a ridge. Life with Tequila increasingly encompassed a return to the spiritual wholeness that I had left behind when my career took over.

Another unanticipated benefit to the move was that Tequila soon became the only horse in the barn with his own private turnout field! As a result of my daily presence at the barn, I struck up a friendship with Ben and Mary Franklin, a retired couple who owned the farm next door. Ben had been a frequent visitor to the Polo Club, a tall, lean, good-looking man who was regarded with some awe. "He owns race horses; he's a partner of Woodrow Marriott," the regulars used to say. One day at the Club, Ben saw me feeding sugar cubes to Tequila. "Never feed a horse sugar," he admonished, "it isn't good for them and gives them worms." Tequila never got another sugar cube.

As we became friends, Ben invited me to graze Tequila in his fields. Ben no longer owned horses, though he had several cows. That posed no problem for Tequila, who was at least part quarter horse; he got along splendidly with cattle. In fact, we spent many happy hours rounding them up and herding them from field to field, often with me along for the ride bareback.

Ben also had a very small bay Shetland pony on the premises, and he thought Tequila's company would be good for her. Little Coco had belonged to his granddaughter. The pony had foundered badly many years before, and now rarely moved beyond the door of her stall. Tequila quickly changed that.

Within a few months, we had a routine worked out. In exchange for caring for Coco and the cows, I could turn Tequila out every day in Ben's ample pastures. I could leave him there all day if I wanted to, or turn him out overnight in the summer. With the little pony at his side, and plenty of grass and a pond, he was perfectly happy with the arrangement; it was the only field from which he never escaped. Coco also was much happier, and began venturing out to graze with her new friend. It was a heartwarming sight to see Tequila go to her stall, nuzzle her up, and push her gently across the field.

Tequila thrived on the longer turnout and our daily trail rides. As we moved into the shorter days of fall and winter, and the evening hours grew darker, I started arriving at the barn in the mornings before work as well: I could turn him out, or even do a short 20 minute trail ride through the woods, then change clothes in the barn office and drive to meet my bus. I stopped taking riding lessons; Tequila became my instructor, a role he would play for the rest of his life. That year, for the first time, when co-workers would inquire about my vacation plans, I said I didn't need to take a vacation: I had one every day, when I rode my horse.

There were, of necessity, certain tradeoffs in the new arrangement. I was not available any more for "spur of the moment" evenings at the Kennedy Center. There were no more dinners in downtown restaurants. I began to lose contact with some of my "non-horse" friends. But Washington is always a city in flux: with each election, old friends leave and new people arrive to take their place. It is a city of constant "hellos" and "goodbyes." Most of my friends remained friends: we met for lunch, or they would take a mini-holiday and come out to the country for dinner or a picnic at the barn. In addition, I was making new and wonderful friends among my riding companions at the barn.

The move also required me to make other financial arrangements for Tequila. Some years before, I had named two college classmates – my friend Owen and my lawyer Marty – as executors of my estate. When Tequila entered my life, we devised an agreement that the funds in my savings account would be used to care for Tequila if anything happened to me. Now, with the purchase of my house, I had no savings left! Marty drew up another document designating the funds in my retirement account as a maintenance fund for Tequila, to be administered by himself and Owen. He then drew up a second document, an official-looking contract between the owners of Stoneridge and me, guaranteeing that as long as Tequila lived he would have his stall and proper daily care. Tequila was now the only horse in the barn with a legal contract and a trust fund!

As carefully as we plan our lives, however, life has a way or surprising us. Just when I thought we had a system that would work forever – or at least for the next several years – nature tossed us a curve ball. I knew Tequila wasn't indestructible, but at the relatively young age of 15 or 16, I thought he had many more years to go before age and infirmity caught up with him. After all, he was the fastest racer, the best jumper, the liveliest horse in the barn.

Then, on one of our daily trail rides, as we crossed a rocky stream, Tequila pulled up acutely lame. It was his right front foot, and it would plague him, and me, for the rest of his life. At first the resident veterinarian diagnosed a probable stone bruise, and I rested him for a few days. But when I turned him out again, he was still lame in that foot.

The blacksmith pulled the shoe, and we quickly discovered the problem: an abscess in the "white line" just at the break-over point in his toe. That is the place in the front of the toe which bears the full weight as the horse steps forward and moves into the next stride. It is the point of maximum stress, because it is stretched with every step the horse takes. The veterinarian was called in again, and prescribed antibiotics. I began a regimen of soaking Tequila's foot twice a day in hot Epsom Salt to draw out the infection. Was I ever grateful at that point that I had made the decision to move to Great Falls.

Everyone assured me that an abscess was "nothing to worry about." "It's a long way from his heart," was the way the owner of the barn phrased it. "It will clear up in a couple weeks and he'll be good as new." Wrong! Though he would enjoy long periods of soundness, and though there were thousands of miles of trail rides in our future, the little abscess that we discovered on July 10, 1980, would never completely go away.

I began to learn some very important lessons. I learned first of all that injuries can take a long time to heal. We would treat the problem for a few weeks, soaking every day, then re-shoe with a pad to keep the dirt out and think he would be fine. A week later he would be lame again. We would drill out the infection and clean the cavity and think we had the spot immaculate and nothing could possibly be left in it. Then we would fill the hole with acrylic, re-shoe, and two weeks later the stubborn bacteria would be back and Tequila would be lame again. We would put him on a heavy dose of antibiotics for two weeks and think no bacteria could possibly survive the dosage, and three weeks later the abscess would recur.

I learned to look for the warning signs: a bit of warmth in his hoof, a slightly elevated pulse to his right front foot, a reluctance to go out on the trail of an evening. The latter was a sure sign that something was wrong, because Tequila normally always wanted to go. In the end, he became my best guide to his condition: if he didn't want to jump, if he started out on the trail and wanted to come back, I knew beyond a shadow of a doubt that there was a problem. As time went on, I became as attuned to his body as I was to my own. I also was beginning to realize how much commitment is involved in the word "love."

As we grew together, I became increasingly aware that there were special moments that I wanted to remember. I began making notes: of an exciting outing, a thunderstorm, a quiet moment in the barn, a special communion in the field.

One evening when we were riding at dusk, trotting around the edge of a big field, we came upon three bucks grazing in the tall grass. One was an eight-pointer; the other two were ten-pointers; and they usually are among the flightiest of animals. This time, however, they looked up, saw Tequila, and accepted him as one of their own; they made no move as we passed within ten feet of them. They just looked. And when I let Tequila stop to graze, they resumed eating as well.

There was the warm spring morning when I had taken a day off from work. I was lying in the grass in Ben's field while Tequila grazed nearby. I was quietly aware that he was moving closer to me, but I never expected him to come and lie down beside me. Contentedly, he stretched out in the grass, groaned happily, lifted his head to catch one last bite of grass, and quietly went to sleep.

There were other times in that field which were not so restful. Tequila loved to play, and I was his favorite playmate – his "preferred companion," as horse psychologists phrase it. We invented our own games. Tequila always started the process. He would come looking for me with a particularly eager, expectant look in his eyes. Sometimes he would whinny or bang on the gate. When I joined him in the field, he would start to buck and prance, then trot around me in a circle and toss his head. I would lunge at him, and we were off!

Despite our mutual middle age, we were like crazy kids. We would race up and down the field, chase each other in circles, run toward each other and veer off at the last minute. Of course he could cover a lot more ground than I could, and often he would be at the top of the hill while I was still scrambling up the base. I would look at him then, a vibrant golden silhouette, neck arched, tail high, an excited whinny calling to the world, "Look at me!"

The game could last two minutes or ten, but it always ended with the two of us trotting side by side, and a pause while he rested his head on my shoulder or nuzzled and licked my hand before he resumed grazing.

There was one night when I arrived at the barn after work and turned him out only to find him a little more exuberant than usual. We had already done a trail ride that morning, so this was to be a "night off." After an hour or so, he came galloping up to the gate. I went to see what he wanted, and he took off bucking, kicking, galloping and snorting. I decided that with that much energy, he needed another ride.

He stood quietly as I mounted bareback, with a halter and leadline to guide him. The minute I was up, however, he became a horse possessed.

He pranced and jigged and tossed his head. My solution to that problem was to put him into a gallop, thinking it would settle him down. He took off like a shot, galloped across the field, then stopped, bucked sky high, landed stiff-legged like a rodeo bronco, and repeated the process until I obligingly came off. He was thoughtful enough to pick a pile of oak leaves, and as I landed on my back I shouted at him, "You brat!"

He trotted off a short distance, and stood there. I could swear he was laughing at me. I quietly took him by the leadline, led him up to the barn, and put a saddle and bridle on him. Even if it WAS getting dark, we were going for a trail ride. He loved it. He didn't want to come back. We picked a very familiar trail, and trotted and cantered and jumped the fallen logs. When we finally returned to the barn in the pitch dark, I turned him out in the field and he took off bucking and galloping again. I watched with pride and awe: my little miracle horse.

Increasingly, Tequila chose the route for our daily trail rides. It always varied, and it always lasted just about an hour. Sometimes he would opt for the "galloping field," and we would tear around that mile course several times before jumping the creek and heading back through the woods to home. Other times he would want to go at a quiet trot through the woods, and we would follow the trail along Nichol's

Run until it veered up a steep hill and came out in a lush pasture. I let him do it. It was fun for ME to see where he would take me, and it was an intense pleasure to know that he was doing what he wanted to do.

It was on one of those rides that he first showed me what I came to call his "overdrive." It was an incredible gait, when his whole body flattened toward the ground and his legs stretched out both in front and back until it seemed that his feet left the ground. It was as if he became a living trajectory; it was a lot like flying. And while I experienced it many more times on our rides together, I never actually SAW it happen until the Kentucky Derby of 2001, when a lovely gray horse named Monarchos, as he approached the finish line, flattened and dropped his body close to the ground and flew like an arrow to his goal.

Many of my rides with Tequila were nothing short of spectacular. One particularly memorable Christmas Eve, just before the ground froze for the winter, Tequila and I had been on a long ride, visiting places that might not be accessible again until Spring. We had stopped at our favorite place in the stream; it was already half iced-over. We had trotted and cantered and galloped and jumped, something we could not do once the ground froze hard.

At last, it was time to come home. The sun had set. Dark clouds were moving in that would soon drop snow and sleet on the woods and fields. Worst of all, we could sense a cold front on the way. We rode along in silence, stepping gingerly along trails that already were half-frozen mud.

As we came off one trail onto a gravel road, Tequila stopped and stared. The white gateposts of a large house were before us, their lamps lit in the twilight, and hanging beneath each lamp was a large green wreath with a fluttering red bow.

Tequila had an appropriate sense of wonder, and of curiosity. He walked to the nearest gatepost and put his nose on the wreath. He sniffed the balsam branches and nuzzled the velvet bow. His sense of wonder was matched by my own, as I gazed at the beautiful palomino horse in the lamplight, dark eyes wide, ears perked, nuzzling a Christmas wreath on a frosty night. In a life which was filled with wondrous images, it was a moment of unparalleled beauty, that filled my heart with thanks for the gift I had been given.

The next day was almost as grand, but in a very different way. Christmas Day dawned windy, cold, dark and threatening. The ground was covered with a snowy mix, and the temperature was already in the 20s and plunging. I turned Tequila out in the field, and watched in amazement as he bucked and galloped and played. The ground was not yet fully frozen. I knew instantly what we would do.

Instead of a walk/trot trail ride through the woods

as I had planned, we would cross the main road and head for an open stretch of fields. It is not a route we often took, paralleling a busy street and passing in front of a new housing development. But this day I knew that the grass would cushion the freezing ground, and we would be able to do one last gallop.

As I saddled up, I sensed that Tequila had the same idea: he was ready to go. He pranced from the very first, picked up a trot, and then the gallop burst from him like a shot. We galloped to the end of the field; we turned and galloped back. A sand truck backfired behind us and Tequila hurled into a gallop once again. Still again, we raced the nearly half mile to the new Catholic Church, then back again. He raced so fully, so freely, and with such joyful abandon!

Back at the barn I laughed, hugged my horse, and gave thanks to God for the best Christmas gift of all: Tequila's health, his high spirits, and the joy and wonder that he brought to my life.

It was about this time that Tequila began following me back to the barn when it was time for our trail ride. I could turn him out in Ben's field all day, and when I went to get him for the evening, I didn't need to bring a halter and a leadline. Tequila would eagerly cross the pasture with me, halt on command at the gate, pick up a trot if we were running late. I would open the gate and turn him loose, tell him to wait while I closed and latched it, and he would follow me into the barn to be brushed and saddled.

There was one night, however, when this routine did NOT work. Tequila was out in the field when a thunderstorm came up. I borrowed a dark blue slicker from the pile by the barn door and went out to get him. He started toward me. But as soon as he got within range, he sniffed, and his attitude changed. He jerked away, pinned his ears, wheeled and threatened to kick. Every time I tried to touch him he got increasingly irritated, and the kicks got increasingly close. Finally, I figured it out: he smelled other horses on me. I removed the slicker and tossed it as far as I could across the field, and was rewarded immediately with a nuzzle, and a horse who walked quietly beside me back to the barn.

As our mutual trust grew, and my confidence grew with it, we ranged farther and farther afield. We rode to the Potomac River; we took all-day excursions to destinations where we had never ventured before. I was warned that it was risky going out alone, and these outings were not without their occasional mishaps.

Once, miles from home, we rode down to a stream just as two riders approached from the opposite direction. We entered the water at the same time and exchanged greetings. Then I noticed something that seemed amiss, and said to the two other riders: "Do you know that both of your bridles have slipped over one ear?" I had never seen Western tack before, and didn't realize that these were Western bridles that were supposed to fit over just one ear! But Tequila acted like he knew. As if on cue, he shook his head, dropped to his knees, and lay down in the stream – a picture of total embarrassment. There I was, still in the saddle, and up to my waist in water. At that point it was hard to tell which of us was the more embarrassed.

Another all-day excursion took us to the Potomac River. As we cantered along a stretch of the shore, a trail that branched off to the right and up a hill caught Tequila's eye. With no warning, he veered and took off at a gallop for the top of that hill. Unfortunately for me, there was a big oak tree with a low branch overhanging the trail. Foolishly, in those days I did not ride with a hard hat, and I could neither halt Tequila nor duck far and fast enough. I caught the branch full on my forehead. The force lifted me out of the saddle, over Tequila's rump, and left me lying unconscious on my back with my head pointing down the trail.

When I came to, Tequila was standing over me, looking puzzled: he had made it under, why hadn't I? I sat up gingerly, found my sunglasses, and felt blood streaming down my face. Tying my bandanna over the wound, I remounted and headed for home. After a mile or two we passed another boarding stable, where two other riders got a look at me. "Do you want us to drive you home, and we can trailer your horse?" they wanted to know. "That's OK, he can get me home," was the reply that brought stares of amazement. It was another four miles back to our own barn, but Tequila did, indeed, get me safely home. I had a bit of a headache the next day, and I drew a few comments on the commuter bus, but the next night we were back on the trail.

It was not long after this that a rider in Great Falls was killed when her horse spooked and threw her as they were crossing a road. Many sports are dangerous: skiing, skydiving, motorcycle and car racing, to name a few. But in only one sport are there TWO minds involved, which must be operating in tandem at all times. Horseback riding has rightly been classified as the most dangerous sport there is, and it behooves every participant to take full precautions.

By this time, I had been riding for five years. I was almost 40 years old. I had suffered several broken bones and been knocked unconscious twice. As important as it was to care for my horse, it was also important to care for myself. I had always observed certain precautions, paying close attention to weather and to possibly dangerous footing. I knew the importance of keeping my bridle and saddle in good condition and regularly checking the leather for wear. Except when I was riding bareback, I knew enough to use proper attire: boots with ankle supports and heels that wouldn't slip through the stirrups, chaps or riding britches for good contact with the saddle, and sometimes even gloves for gripping the reins. But I had always resisted wearing a hard hat – I just didn't like the way it looked. Finally, that too became regular attire, though I insisted on dressing it up with different colored covers to match my outfits.

As Tequila grew older, a hoof abscess was not his only problem. He also developed arthritis. Like the abscess, the onset was very sudden. We were riding along the stream one day when he unexpectedly came up lame in his left hind leg. I thought he had somehow pulled a muscle, though I could find no heat or swelling or sensitivity anywhere in that leg. I walked him back and found the owner of the barn, who was giving a lesson in the ring. I asked her to watch while I trotted him in the ring, to see if she could see the problem.

Tequila, as usual, had his own ideas of what was appropriate and what was not, and doing anything in a ring after a long trail ride was definitely NOT appropriate. However, there were people watching, so he did what seemed natural to him. He put on a show! When I asked for a trot, he broke into a canter and headed straight for the biggest jump in the ring. It was a rail across a row of oil drums which he easily cleared. Then, having done what he thought he should do, he trotted to the gate and stood waiting for me to praise him and give him treats.

Based on that brief observation, my colleagues agreed that it was probably a pulled leg muscle. The first veterinarian who examined him diagnosed the seemingly ubiquitous "stone bruise." Give him a few days rest and start riding again was the advice I was given. But the lameness kept recurring, sporadic, but disturbing. Once again, I called on "Dr. Dave," who several years before had gotten out of the horse business and was now strictly a small-animal vet.

Dave hadn't seen Tequila in years, but he watched me walk him out of the barn and pronounced, "He has arthritis from his loose stifles." The stifle is a hind leg joint that is the equivalent of the knee joint in a human. And like the knee, it is both complex and relatively unstable. A loose stifle means that the joint is subject to more wear than normal; the ligaments may become a bit stretched, and the bones are prone to rub. Dave also remembered that Tequila had been lame in that leg several years before, a fact that I had forgotten, but which was later confirmed in his notes. Age and wear had in fact resulted in arthritis. Dave recommended that I put him on "bute," or butezolidin, a standard anti-inflammatory medication. Within two days, Tequila was trotting sound, and easily broke into a gallop when I mounted him bareback.

But arthritis doesn't clear up that easily. In fact, it doesn't "clear up" at all. As in humans, it is a chronic condition. And it took us several months of experimentation to learn how to keep it under control.

I learned, literally through trial and error, that

the first and most important step is prevention: keep the joint from becoming inflamed in the first place. I learned to keep Tequila on a permanent low maintenance dose of the anti-inflammatory drug. Taking him off the medication only allowed the inflammation to come back. I also learned that when he DID experience a flare-up, the solution was to medicate him strongly at the beginning; give him four pills a day and gradually reduce the dosage rather than gradually increasing the dosage to find an amount that would work.

I began to read a lot about stifles. Conventional wisdom dictated that the stifle is a virtually indestructible joint: unlike the human knee, the stifle is tucked up where the hind leg meets the horse's body, and where it has a lot of protection. "If loose stifles is your horse's only problem, count your blessings," stated one expert on the subject. As I read, I learned that loose stifles is a fairly common problem in horses, and where there is looseness in any joint, the potential for aggravation is very high.

I also learned that arthritic joints should be exercised every day, and I learned that they need flexing and a warm-up period before any vigorous exercise. Finally, Tequila and I had a medical reason for our preferred regimen. If he had been in his stall for the day, I now knew I HAD to turn him out for a while, to let him move around and graze and buck and roll before we went on a trail ride. I also knew that I HAD to ride him every day, and for most of the last half of his life, that is exactly what we did.

Despite the wear and tear on his body, Tequila did not slow down. Of course there were days when his arthritis bothered him, or when the abscess flared up. On those days we took quiet walks in the woods, with plenty of time along the way to graze in a field. But most of his days were good, and on his good days, it always paid to be alert.

Tequila always loved to race. Normally I rode alone for that reason: it was safer, both for me and for other riders. Alone, Tequila could go for miles at a comfortable walk or trot, occasionally breaking into a canter or an exuberant gallop up a hill. But let him hear the first beat of a canter anywhere in the vicinity, and he was OFF! The sound seemed to stir something deep within him: a sense of survival, a love of adventure, a joy of speed, a zest for competition. Many is the time on a trail ride that a horse has cantered to catch up with Tequila, and found itself caught in a hell-bent-for-leather dash that it could never hope to win.

Tequila never came in second. On one memorable spring day, four riders from Stoneridge caught up with us in our "galloping field." They were all riding big 16-hand bay thoroughbreds, and as they emerged from the woods behind us, Tequila heard them and took off. They joined the fun, but they got left behind in the dust. We raced around the field three times, Tequila always in the lead, and he finished the race half a field ahead of them.

One of his most impressive performances occurred on a Sunday morning. It had been raining for days, and the world had turned to mud. I met a fellow boarder out on a trail ride, and together we discovered a road that had been bulldozed out of the forest and had not yet been surfaced. It was over a mile of virgin mud. We let our horses break into a canter, and the race was on.

Tequila surged ahead, and held the lead in a display of skill that a professional jockey would have envied. He conserved his strength in the taxing footing, keeping just ahead of his rival. He cut the other horse off on the turns, veered in front to block its path, slowed slightly until the other horse started to gain and then blasted out in front again. He won easily: against a thoroughbred mare six inches taller than himself, four years younger, and a half-sister to the incomparable Secretariat.

Tequila pranced a little at the end, as well he might, then he insisted on taking the lead on the way home. He was boss, and he meant to show it.

Tequila had one habit on a trail ride that drives most riders crazy: he liked to eat as we went along. If he had been kept in his stall all day, there was no way I wanted to fight with him the entire ride to keep him from nibbling at the branches. If he wanted a bite or two of grass when we slowed up from a long trot, I allowed it. I indulged his habit because it heightened his enjoyment of the outing.

There were times, however, when his indulgences were quite remarkable. Passing beside a cornfield, he was not above uprooting a stalk of corn and walking along contentedly munching on it, while I hoped fervently that no one would notice. Branches occasionally fell into his grasp, and he was known to grab a particularly succulent clump of orchard grass in his teeth in mid-stride at a full gallop.

One particular experience still makes me smile. It happened one evening when the owner of the barn was taking a group of children on their first trail ride. She was instructing them on trail etiquette, which of course included: "Don't let your horse eat while you are riding him." All of a sudden the class burst out laughing, and Sharon looked up the trail to see Tequila and me coming down the hill toward her. Tequila was dragging an entire small tulip tree, contentedly munching its leaves as he walked along.

Our life together was not all gallops and snacks, however. We shared other pleasures on our trail rides, and one of the best was a summertime custom of stopping in a cold stream. It began routinely enough: I would let Tequila pause for a drink of water on a hot day. Gradually, our time by the water grew longer; he would stand in the stream with the cooling flow around his feet and legs. I would sit on the bank and watch him, enjoying the soothing sound of the water rippling over the rocks. Then I started loosening his girth, and that evolved into removing his saddle and bridle. Next I began to remove my own boots and socks and join him in the stream. Before we knew it, we were spending literally hours in our "special place," keeping cool on hot summer days. Many was the time that another rider would pass and stare in amazement, at a totally loose horse and a barefoot rider, enjoying a candy bar or an apple in perfect peace.

One of those days was particularly memorable for what I did NOT do. I had been invited to a very special gathering: my former employer, Senator Edward W. Brooke, was having a staff reunion at his new farm in Warrenton, to celebrate his 65th birthday. Former colleagues and friends were coming from all over the country. I had my hair done especially for the occasion, I had a new pickup truck I wanted to show off, and I was looking forward to it. But it was a hot day, and the stream was cool, and the companionship with Tequila was soothing. We stayed in the stream. The hour grew late. As the sun began to fade, I reconciled myself to the fact that I would never make it to the party. And the Senator, sounding very much like my mother, reportedly told the other guests: "She is probably with that horse." He was right. I did not regret the choice.

As my relationship with Tequila developed, it was only natural that I would become curious about his origins. I had wondered from the very beginning where he came from, what his breeding was, what his past experiences were. The explanation offered by the manager of the Polo Club - that he was "by truck out of Front Royal" - was not the answer I was looking for! All I knew for sure was that he had belonged to a teenager in Great Falls, who sold him to the Polo Club when she went off to college. But where did SHE get him? And what did she do with him when she had him?

I decided to seek some answers, and began by posting a picture of him on the bulletin board at the Saddlery in Great Falls. I was curious to see if anyone would recognize him. I didn't have long to wait! The calls started coming in the very next day. When I expressed surprise at the response, one caller said, "He's pretty hard to forget!" And she wasn't referring just to his unusual coloring.

I heard from his previous owner, a young woman named Kathy, and from her friend Janean. As teenagers, the two of them had many adventures: Kathy on Tequila, whom she had named Marengo, and Janean on her chocolate palomino, Pepper. I heard stories of how the two girls would let their horses gallop for miles, until one of the other horse finally had enough. I heard how they would ride their horses along Difficult Run to Great Falls Park, where they would entertain visitors by jumping over picnic tables. No wonder Tequila had come to hate his time of stall confinement and ring lessons at the Polo Club!

One day Kathy came out to Stoneridge to see Tequila. Now a mature young woman with a boyfriend in tow, she gave him an apple, patted his neck, and called him "Old Man." I knew Tequila recognized her, but I was selfishly pleased that he showed no special bond. He was strictly my horse now.

From one caller who had worked at the barn where Kathy boarded him years before, I heard hair-raising tales about Tequila's legendary independence. I was told, for example, that every morning when the horses were turned out for the day, Tequila would canter straight to the fence, sail over it, and head down Walker Road – one of the two main roads running through the town of Great Falls. I learned that he would simply trot off wherever his whimsy took him. Sometimes he would see another horse grazing in a field, and jump into the field for a social call. Sometimes he would simply jump a fence and graze on the other side for a while. Neighbors grew accustomed to the sight, and stopped calling to report a "loose horse."

Part of his motivation, I suspect, is that he never did enjoy grazing with a herd of horses; he was a little horse, and I don't think he ever felt secure in a crowd. Mostly, however, I think he just had supreme confidence and a love of adventure. Wherever his wanderings took him, he was always back for dinner. The stable hand had only to rattle a feed bucket, and Tequila would jump back INTO the pasture and be first in line for the food.

One woman who boarded at the same barn in those days had this description of Tequila: "He was always incredibly independent. He was also the best jumper I've ever seen. He jumped like a deer. He would canter to the fence – always the highest part – collect himself just as if he had a rider telling him what to do, bring his legs under him, and sail over."

People never forgot Tequila. One day, about ten years after I brought him back to Great Falls, I was riding on the edge of a field. A woman approached from the other direction, riding a big chestnut gelding. We exchanged pleasantries, and as we passed, Tequila reached over to sniff the other horse. "Take it easy there, Marengo," the woman said. It came out as effortlessly as if she had just seen him the day before, and I rode on in awe of the impression he must have made on her.

Not long after that I had another, similar experience. A new employee came to work at Stoneridge, a young woman named Kelli, who had been hired to do the morning feeding and turnouts. I introduced myself, and then she looked at Tequila. "You haven't always been at this barn, have you?" she queried. "Didn't this horse used to be at the Reston Polo Club? Isn't he the one who used to jump out of his stall?" I smiled. Tequila certainly did leave a lasting impression.

Another person who will never forget Tequila is an accomplished horsewoman named Robin Sabin, who served for many years as the District Head of the Pony Club. Robin considered me an experienced rider, and occasionally invited me to trail ride with her.

One of our first outings was along Difficult Run to the Potomac River. Robin had a new mare fresh off the track that she was breaking in to trail ride, and she thought the company of a seasoned trail horse would be good for her mare. We trailered to our starting point, saddled up, and set off on the five-mile trip to the river. Tequila claimed the lead, and held it, heading the mare off at every turn. We walked and trotted through beautiful woods blooming with mountain laurel. The stream was full from the spring rains and we rode to the sound of the flowing water and the call of the birds. After an hour or so, we came to the river, a wide expanse of blue alive with waterfowl: ducks, geese, herons and occasional hawks.

Tequila had behaved well, and as we turned for home, I asked Robin if I could give him "a little gallop" without upsetting her mare. The answer was affirmative. I said the magic word, "OK," and Tequila was off like greased lightning. Trees became a blur. Water was something we splashed through, or leaped over without even touching. By my best reckoning, we galloped for three miles. We were half an hour ahead of Robin getting back to the trailer. "He certainly dominates a trail ride, doesn't he?" was her breathless comment when she finally caught up.

A few months later, Robin and I set out on another adventure. This time she brought her most experienced hunter. We chose a site near Bull Run Park in Prince William County. Tequila always loved new places, and by the time we arrived he was clearly excited. We tacked up and started out on our ride, and very quickly I informed Robin that I would have to let Tequila have a gallop "to settle him down." As usual, it did the opposite; it got him more revved up.

We rode happily through woods and fields, exploring the territory, surprising the deer, crossing and re-crossing Bull Run. But while Robin was enjoying the view of the distant Blue Ridge Mountains, I was trying to maintain SOME control over my horse.

Tequila was used to making all the decisions on a trail ride. At one point, he very definitely wanted to go in one direction, while Robin and I wanted to go in the other. Each time I tried to turn him, he would wheel and head in the opposite direction. We must have circled 15 or 20 times, with Robin laughing out loud and saying, "I've seen riders circle their horses for discipline, but I've never seen a horse circle a rider for discipline!"

Eventually, we compromised. We picked up a new trail, rode around a field, had a good long gallop, then plunged down an embankment and crossed the stream. After an hour and a half, it was time to head home. But Tequila didn't want to go home. There were still new trails and fields to explore, and he wanted to keep going.

I decided to let him gallop back to the trailer, to see if that would satisfy him. We took off up and down some hills, crossing one gravel road in a single leap. At the top of the next hill we could see the trailer – but Tequila still wasn't finished. He veered to the right and went out across yet another range of hills.

Finally, we halted. Robin, meanwhile, had sensibly cantered her horse back to the trailer, and there in the distance I could see her waiting for us. Tequila, for one of the few times in his life, was breathing hard. He called to his companion, and set out at a trot and a canter to catch up. When we got back to the trailer, I untacked him, walked him around for a while to cool him off, and we reloaded and drove back to Great Falls, Robin commenting all the way that she'd never seen anything like him. "It's a good thing Tequila found you," she said, "because no one else would put up with him." At the same time, she acknowledged the importance of enjoying what you do, and expressed wonder that Tequila enjoyed his life as much as he did.

I was always proud of the fact that Tequila enjoyed his work. No one else that I knew had a horse who ASKED to be taken out and ridden. Tequila would wait anxiously for me to return at the end of the day, pounding the side of his stall in anticipation. If he was turned out for the day, he would be waiting at the gate when I arrived, ready for his daily adventure.

I have seen so many horses who resist their riders. They swish their tails, or fight the bit, or pull back and try to get away. They inflate their stomachs deliberately so the rider can't tighten the girth. Once out on the trail; they try every subterfuge to turn around and head back home, My little horse never did that.

He showed his pleasure in a multitude of ways. For one thing, he loved to show off. One morning as we came out of the woods there were several new horses grazing in a nearby field. Most horses would stop to visit, to check out other members of their species. Not Tequila. As we approached the fence, I sank my heels a little deeper and started to hunker into the saddle. The new horses were hanging over the fence anticipating a greeting. Instead, Tequila spun 90 degrees and launched himself up the hill with a series of bucks and a long-reaching gallop. When we reached the top, he bucked once more, and his expression said, as plain as any speech, "I showed them that time, didn't I!"

Tequila was satisfied, and he showed it. He tossed his head and snorted, shook his body a bit (yes, I was still in the saddle), pranced into a trot, then found a succulent plant and treated himself to a snack. He had won again. And he knew that he was headed home, where an apple, a roll in the grass, and some grazing time awaited him.

Is it any wonder that a horse communicator who

visited the barn one time, stopped in front of Tequila's stall and said to the barn owner in awe, "This is the most secure horse I have ever seen."

I would like to be able to say that Tequila was always happy, that his time with me always went smoothly. Of course, such was not the case. Once Tequila was REALLY mad, and I recorded the event as it happened.

It began with the first Monday of Daylight Savings Time, when his routine was upset because everything was happening an hour earlier than usual. I rode him earlier in the morning, put him back in his stall an hour earlier than usual, and then returned to the barn an hour earlier in the afternoon. To compound his list of grievances, I had visitors that night. I turned him out in the field while my friends and I sat on the grass, talking and laughing - a conversation of which Tequila was not a part. With each bite of grass, he grazed closer and closer to us, trying to get my attention.

When it was time to bring him in, I tied him in front of his stall where I always groomed him and where he could sniff the dinner waiting in his feed bucket. But my friends wanted to see the new indoor ring, and the rebuilt stalls in the back barn, and Tequila stood waiting while I showed them around.

I gave him hay; he tossed it across the aisle. He pawed impatiently, digging a huge hole in the dirt aisle of the barn. He lifted another horse's blanket off the blanket rack with his teeth and flung THAT across the aisle. I gave him more hay, and that, too, went sailing across the barn. By now his ears were pinned back, his nose was sniffing the food in his bucket, and he was MAD. By the time I brushed him and opened his stall door, he literally flew through the door. There were no gentle rubs, no nuzzles, that night. Tequila wasn't speaking to me.

It was with some trepidation that I returned to the barn the next morning. I knew my horse well enough to know that he would not "forget" overnight. I was right. There was no welcoming nicker when I arrived. No little golden head appearing over the top of the stall. No soft brown eyes were watching for me. "Is anyone here?" I asked rhetorically. BAM! He landed a direct kick on his stall door. I laughed. I knew what he was thinking: "Where do you think I am, you bloody fool?" It was not until after an hour's trail ride, when he galloped and galloped and bucked humongous bucks and worked off all his frustration, that he finally relaxed, nuzzled my hand, and we were friends again.

In those days there was an old man in the county who used to give hay rides to children. He had a wagon and two old horses, and he would travel to Sully Plantation, or a fireman's picnic, or a Fourth of July celebration, and take the children for hay rides. He didn't have a trailer; he was too poor for that. He simply drove his rig up the highway, and stabled his horses overnight at some friendly farm.

One night he stayed with my friend Ben. Tequila was grazing in the front field that night, with a couple of his "buddies." Ben and the old man were leaning on the fence, watching us and talking. They were talking about Tequila. The old man expressed his admiration for Tequila's looks and spirit. Then he turned to Ben and said: "If I had a horse like that, I wouldn't want anything else in the world." I was both deeply touched, and deeply grateful that he was mine.

A PLACE FOR YOU

"Thou anointest my head with oil; my cup overflows."

Psalm 23

As wonderful as our days at Stoneridge were, I had known almost from the beginning that they were numbered. By the 1980s, Great Falls was the last mostly rural community in Fairfax County, and it was undergoing massive development. Fields were being bulldozed to make way for huge homes which we derisively dubbed "McMansions." Inviting trails were being fenced off by new owners who feared liability if horses or riders were injured on their property. The woods directly behind the barn were destined for a housing development, and the time would come when it would be impossible even to cross our favorite stream. The community was running out of trails, and neither Tequila nor I could face the prospect of being limited to riding in the ring.

I had always wanted to retire in mid-life and have a second career as a writer. With Tequila in my life, I had a double incentive to give up the long hours of a Government job. Several years before, I had begun looking for a quiet farm where I could indulge my dream, and provide a permanent home for my beloved horse. I looked forward to the day when there would be no more worries about commuter traffic – or closed trails, or schedule conflicts. I was looking for the next Promised Land.

I took a rather circuitous route, but eventually I found it. My first attempt was in 1978, when I answered a newspaper advertisement for land at an equestrian center near Martinsburg, West Virginia. It was a beautiful place, located on an oxbow of the Potomac River, and the developer had begun by erecting a 65-stall barn with an attached Olympic-sized riding ring. It met my goals of having complete riding facilities available, permanent trails, and eventually a community of other horses and riders. The one thing that I had not considered was its relative isolation; but clearly, other people did; none of the lots sold. The big barn sat empty, and eventually I sold my parcel and looked elsewhere.

My next purchase, in 1984, was closer to home, in Haymarket, Virginia. Here, too, the developer put up a big professional barn and an ornate riding ring. He parceled off the land in ten-acre plots, and as each plot sold he installed three-board fence, included in the purchase price.

This time, at least, I had a fenced in field to start with, and once again I could build a house and barn to my own, and Tequila's, specifications. I think Tequila and I both would have been happy there; at least it wasn't isolated. It was, in fact, right in the heart of the Virginia horse country, with plenty of professional support and wonderful trails to ride.

However, the developer went bankrupt; and I was left holding some lovely property in a very desirable neighborhood indeed. It wasn't long before another developer wanted the land, and I better than "doubled my money."

At that point, not only was I better off financially than when I started, but I had learned more valuable lessons. I began looking seriously for an independent place, not tied to an equestrian community or to another person's finances. Still, it had to be a place that could offer the full support system that Tequila and I would need: good veterinarians and blacksmiths and a good trail network for him; a good library, access to Washington and to my friends, decent shopping and a supportive community for me. As I narrowed my search, I increasingly focused on Warrenton, Virginia.

I loved the town of Warrenton, with its quaint Main Street, its Civil War courthouse, its thriving community life and its deep sense of history. It was also reasonably close to Washington and was home to many retired Foreign Service and government workers, including my former boss, Senator Brooke.

I began looking in earnest, enlisting the help of a wonderful real estate agent who became my friend. We looked at several properties, but nothing really seemed "right." Then one day she called about a "farmette" that had just come on the market.

We drove down a gravel lane between two stone gateposts marked "Black Horse Farm." The place already had potential. The property in question was nestled in between some smaller houses that lined the road, and a 70-acre farm, named for the fabled Virginia Black Horse Cavalry. The property had a very attractive rambler with a two-car garage, behind which was a three-stall barn, three fenced paddocks, a pond, and a stretch of woods already equipped with a network of trails. Licking Run ran through the back of the property. The land backed up to more woods, and across the street was a 1,000 acre cattle farm which was in the territory of the Casanova Hunt.

The place needed some work. Both the barn and the house were painted a sickly green. The fences were in disrepair and in many places were nothing more than barbed wire. The inside of the house was challenging, with every room painted a different color and carpeted with a different rug. But these were all cosmetic issues which could be addressed in time. Basically, the property had everything I was looking for, and the location and the support network were as good as I would ever find.

I bought it. The date was August 31, 1987. But I wasn't retiring for almost a year and a half, and I certainly wasn't going to commute from Warrenton to Washington every day! With the help of my realtor, I found a property manager, who, in turn, found a family to rent my new farm until I was ready to move in. Things were working out well indeed. Not only did I have my "retirement property" with a useable house and barn already in place, but for the first time I had an income-producing property as well.

There was a one-week gap between the time the previous owners moved out and the renters were scheduled to move in. I decided that was the perfect time to introduce Tequila to his new home. And so, the day after closing, I loaded up my truck with my two cats, their litter boxes and equipment, some clean clothes, a sleeping bag, and food: some canned goods for me, buckets and hay and feed for Tequila. We formed a caravan with a Stoneridge horse trailer carrying Tequila out to visit his new home.

I must have been crazy! There I was in a place where I knew no one, with a horse and two cats, planning to stay for a week. I got Tequila settled in one of the stalls with clean bedding and hay and water, and unloaded the truck. My first clue that all would not be well came when I let the cats out of their carriers in the new house. The previous owners had a dog and the scent was everywhere. My smaller cat went behind the toilet in the mudroom and refused to come out – ever.

Undeterred by this small crisis, I saddled Tequila and we went out exploring. It was a new place for him, and he loved new places. We rode for miles, we galloped, we jumped fallen logs. We didn't know the territory at all and I prayed, sincerely and often, that he would not step in a hole or tangle with a wire fence.

It was dinner time when we returned to the barn, and I groomed and fed and watered him and put him in for the night. I slept on the deck that night, over-looking the barn in case there was a problem. All was quiet until about 4:30 a.m., when I heard the first whinny. I went down to the barn in my night shirt and sandals – after all, these stalls had Dutch doors, which he was certainly capable of jumping. I fed him hay, talked to him, hand grazed him, and kept him company until sunup. Then I made the worst mistake of all: I turned him out in the field. I thought that having good grass to eat might settle him down. I should have known by then that when Tequila is agitated, NOTHING settles him down.

As I watched in horror, Tequila began circling the field, gathering steam as he went. Then in a long sweeping motion, he started at the back of the field, cantered toward the front, and flew over the corner of the front fence that faced on the gravel road. Within seconds he was out of sight, up the hill and onto the paved road.

My first reaction was straight denial: this simply hadn't happened. My horse was not loose 50 miles from home. I would go in the house and fix a cup of tea.

My second reaction was to throw on some clothes, jump in the truck and head up the road in the direction I was sure he had taken: back toward Great Falls. I had visions of him galloping the four miles to the four-lane highway and trying to make it all the way to Great Falls on his own. I was frankly panicked.

As I drove up and down the road, there was no sign of a palomino horse. I began the next phase of the search, pulling in to each driveway to see if by chance he was "visiting" somewhere. It brought back awful memories of our first trail ride at Frying Pan Park, twelve years before, when he had been gone overnight.

Finally, I pulled into one farm just half a mile or so up the road. I was greeted by a puzzled farmer and his very pregnant wife, still in her chenille bathrobe. A horse had suddenly turned up in their yard as the farmer was feeding the cattle, and he had put the horse in the pen and given him some grain. Sure enough, there was Tequila, happily munching away.

I put his halter on and got him away from the corn: on top of everything else, I didn't need him getting sick. With deepest gratitude for his safety, and many reassuring hugs, I led him back to his barn. Then I went to the nearest house, knocked on the door, and asked to use the phone. Fortunately the house also had two young children, who were delighted, indeed, to be asked to come down to my barn and feed a week's supply of carrots to a very pretty horse, simply to keep him quiet. While they plied Tequila with treats, I packed up the cats and the canned goods and my clothes and prepared for the return trip.

The Stoneridge trailer brought us back barely 24 hours after we had left. I turned Tequila out in Ben's field. He nuzzled his pony in greeting, and settled down to graze. The next day, I went back to work. It was a year before I visited the farm again!

Meanwhile, something else was happening in my life. For years, Tequila had taken up so much of my time that dating was out of the question. I had many friends, but no romantic involvement; I truly thought those days were long past. But after I had been at Stoneridge for about 12 years, I started "seeing" one of my fellow Great Falls commuters.

Paul Lawrence first came to my attention as a nice-looking and somewhat mysterious fellow passenger on the Great Falls commuter bus. The bus, the 23X, ran from the "social center" of our community, the Great Falls Safeway, to the West Falls Church Metro stop. There, we would all pile onto the Orange Line train for the trip to downtown Washington, reassembling in the evening for the return home.

Great Falls, in those days, was a relatively small community, and over many years of commuting together, numerous friendships had blossomed. Largely, I confess, at my instigation, we put together a "bus roster" which included addresses, occupations – and birthdays. A number of us began meeting once a month in Washington for a "commuter club" lunch, and birthdays were often raucous evening events aboard the bus with wine and cheese. We included spouses in many of our celebrations, the most memorable of which turned into a surprise birthday party – for me.

In this group of professionals, Paul always stood out. He didn't participate in our social gatherings, and he never mentioned a spouse. While the other men wore business suits, Paul always dressed in khakis and a navy blue blazer. When they wore topcoats or trench coats in the winter, Paul wore a camouflage jacket, with an Australian bush hat. I first noticed him for a very practical reason: I was always the last person to come flying into the parking lot in the morning, straight from the barn; and I never had the right change for the bus. The daily fare was an incomprehensible $1.15. And while I usually had the dollar, the 15 cents was always a problem. Paul carried a leather change purse, and he always offered the nickel or the dime that I needed.

We often talked on the bus; or rather, he talked and I listened. I learned that he was a lawyer with the Civil Rights Division of the Department of Justice. I learned that he was a retired Army colonel: Special Forces, Green Beret, Ranger/ Airborne. That,

I supposed, accounted both for his short haircut and his unusual dress. I learned that there were many times when he was more frightened as a poll watcher in our own deep South than he had ever been in the deep jungles of Vietnam. With my background in civil rights and social justice issues, I found his accounts of the current struggles fascinating. I learned that he also had a Master's degree in International Relations, and he was unquestionably a superb athlete. He didn't talk much about his war experiences, which was just as well at that point in our relationship; I would have found them horrifying, to say the least.

As time wore on, Paul showed a growing interest in becoming better acquainted. He started dropping by the barn in the evenings, keeping me company while Tequila grazed. He was handy around the barn: he helped clean stalls, he got hay down from the loft, he commented somewhat knowledgeably about Tequila's weight or some sign of lameness. After a while, I came to accept his presence, and so did Tequila. It was some time before he told me anything about his personal life. By then he was in the midst of a lengthy divorce.

One night, Paul invited me to his house for dinner. I discovered that he lived in a big, imposing house, with his elderly mother. And I learned that he could cook! One thing led to another, and the schedule that I thought was inflexible began to show some flex. Paul, who took the early bus home, took over the evening tasks at the barn. He would bring Tequila in from the field (or turn him out, depending on the season), groom him, feed him, and clean his stall. By the time I got back to Great Falls around 7 p.m., I would drive to Paul's house where a drink, and dinner, and a fire in the fireplace would be waiting. After an evening with him and his mother, I would drive home. The next morning I would be at the barn at my customary 4:30 or 5 a.m., enjoy my trail ride, and the daily routine would resume.

On weekends, I often rode Tequila in the direction of Paul's house. Two of his grandsons were usually there, and they delighted in seeing my horse. The younger boy, Matthew, then about six or seven years old, loved to get up in the saddle and be led around the yard. And Tequila, who was very kind to children, didn't mind a bit. In fact, there were other children on our route who also became "regulars" for "pony rides," including the two little daughters of another of my bus companions. Children were no threat to Tequila, and they usually carried treats.

It was a pleasant existence, and I was getting used to it. Many years before, in a letter to a cousin, my father had speculated on my marriage prospects: "If Marilyn ever marries, it will be late in life, and it will be to a doctor or lawyer, and it will be for companionship." Maybe, I was beginning to think, my father had been right.

But after a few months, the combined pressures of the divorce proceedings and financial worries began to take their toll on Paul. We "broke up." A few weeks later, we began seeing each other again, but our dinners were less frequent and our weekend outings more limited. I did not give up hope for a more serious relationship, but I went about my life, enjoying the added time with Tequila and making plans for my own retirement at the end of the year.

Then one day, Paul's older sister arrived and took their mother to live with her on the West Coast. A few weeks later, in early July, I arrived at the barn one morning to find two notes from Paul tacked to Tequila's stall door: one for Tequila, and one for me. My note said, basically, "I am leaving and I will not be back." Tequila's note was even more dramatic: "If you see Traveler (Robert E. Lee's famous horse) before I do, give him my regards." No destination was given.

It was a tremendous shock. And, as so many people do in time of grave troubles, I turned to prayer. Appropriately enough, the prayer that sustained me appeared that very day in the Congressional Record. It had been offered the day before by the Rev. James D. Ford, Chaplain of the House of Representatives:

"Your word heals the hurts in the lives of people everywhere, and gives calm and confidence to our lives... . You are always with us to bless us in all the critical moments of life."

I prayed that Paul would find healing. I placed my trust in God's hands. And I got on with my life. In early August, there was an envelope from Paul: no note, no address, just a paper placemat from a diner, showing a map of Puget Sound and a Voice of America transmitter. At least now I knew where he was! Then came a postcard, and a phone call. In late August he asked if I would come out to the West Coast for a visit, so we could talk. I agreed. It was in the course of this visit that we decided that we truly cared for one another and wanted to merge our lives. Paul began making plans to return to Virginia.

But, as I was to learn, life sometimes exacts a toll: there was a tradeoff. The trip to Seattle was the one and only time that I knowingly let Tequila down. A few days before I left, Tequila had stepped on a piece of wire which left a puncture wound in his right front leg. The puncture wasn't visible at first, and I didn't notice anything amiss until one night he came up lame, and I found heat and swelling.

I called the new veterinarians I had begun to use after "Dr. Dave" got out of the horse business for good. They were two very competent young women, recently graduated from veterinary school, and they came out to the barn immediately. "Let's try a sweat wrap to get the swelling down," they suggested. It was the worst thing we could have done. By the next day Tequila's leg had swollen almost twice its normal size, and the heat was unbearable. We stripped off the wraps, and that is when we found the puncture, which we opened, drained, and started Tequila on massive doses of antibiotics.

For a week, the veterinarians came every day to change the dressing and check on his progress. We put a support wrap on his left leg, which was now bearing much of his weight because his right leg was too painful to stand on. Within a couple of days the swelling began to go down, and we were able to take him on short walks to improve the circulation. He was making progress; but he had a ways to go. And I had to leave for Seattle!

I arranged for someone to walk Tequila twice a day while I was gone. I left him in the care of my veterinarians and flew to the West Coast. When I returned, Tequila was much improved; the swelling was almost gone, he was putting equal weight on both front legs. But something else was wrong. He stepped gingerly on the trail ride; he didn't want to trot or canter; he acted like his feet hurt him.

The blacksmith came, and we soon learned the reason for Tequila's unusual reluctance to exercise: he had begun to founder in both front feet, from the stress and the fever.

Founder is a particularly painful, and often fatal, affliction of the hoof. A horse's foot in encased in a hard, solid substance known as the hoof wall. Inside are sensitive connective tissues, and a bone, appropriately called the coffin bone, because of its shape. When the foot becomes inflamed or irritated, there is nowhere for the swelling to go; the hoof wall doesn't "give." The sensitive connective tissue can be displaced by the pressure of the internal swelling, and when that happens the coffin bone, which the tissues have held in place, can actually drop or rotate out of position. In extreme cases the pressure builds up to the point where the hoof wall actually separates from the horse's leg, or the coffin bone comes through the sole of the foot.

Tequila's founder seemed to be fairly slight, and it clearly had stopped by the time the blacksmith found it. But inside both front feet, we knew, were weakened tissues and bones that probably had rotated, if only slightly, out of position.

With trimming and shoeing Tequila rapidly improved, and within a matter of days he was back to normal. The crisis was over for now. And, to be perfectly honest, with everything else that was going on in my life, I soon forgot about it. We resumed our daily rides, our madcap gallops, our joyous jumps; Tequila was himself again; and life was very good,

It was late November of 1988 when Paul returned from Seattle. He pulled his truck straight into the barn, which is where he knew I would be. For the next few weeks he made himself useful: carrying pickup truck loads of our belongings out to the farm; overseeing the construction of the new fencing and the upgrading of the barn, and helping with the care of Tequila. He also indulged in a week of one of his favorite pastimes – deer hunting.

On December 16, 1988, my office gave me a retirement party. About 60 people attended, including friends from the Agency and from Congress. One of the Associate Directors of the Agency made the traditional speech. Only this time he said, "We have all thought of Marilyn as riding off into the sunset – but she will not be riding off alone. She is getting married tomorrow to Col. Paul Lawrence, who is with us today." There were gratifying gasps of surprise from the assembled well-wishers, and not a few exclamations of "Why didn't you tell me?" To this day, I cannot answer that question; maybe, deep down, I always thought it wouldn't happen. But it did.

The very next afternoon, I stood in the living room of my Great Falls home, surrounded by friends and facing a woman marriage celebrant from the Fairfax Court. To the accompaniment of a bagpiper and a flurry of snow, Paul and I became husband and wife.

I was asked numerous times why I didn't have the ceremony at the barn, so Tequila could participate, too. My answer was always the same: I chose not to, out of consideration for Tequila. "He would never have understood why he wasn't the center of attention."

By now my renovated farm was ready for occupancy. The paddocks all had new, sturdy board fencing and new gates. The barn had been strengthened and repaired, with the stalls and Dutch doors built up to a height of eight feet on all sides. Special "horse-proof" bolt latches had been installed on all the stall doors. I had plenty of work done on the house as well, repainting all the rooms in an off-white, and re-carpeting the whole house in soft beige.

We moved in two days before Christmas. Ben gave Coco to Tequila as a going-away present and companion, a gift for which I was eternally grateful. This time, the Stoneridge van carried both equines, and was followed by two pickup trucks carrying Paul, my two cats, and me. My new family was already growing!

Everything went smoothly, but I was taking no chances. For the first few days, until I was sure he was settled in, I handgrazed Tequila for hours. But this time the things around him were familiar, and he had his pony with him. He quickly adjusted to his new home. He particularly came to enjoy one feature that was of special importance to both of us: the stall doors facing the field stayed open when the horses were turned out. They were free, at last, to go in and out, to escape bad weather or bugs, to take a nap whenever they wished in the shade on their soft bedding. At their age, it was a luxury they deserved.

There was one further addition to our family that first winter. About two weeks after we had moved in, I got a call from the owner of Stoneridge. "Wimpy won't eat, and he sits at the head of the drive all day looking for you. Do you want him?" Wimpy was my favorite barn cat, a long-haired black and white beast who had adopted both Tequila and me. He slept in the loft over Tequila's stall; he ate his meals – canned tuna – on the hood of my truck. It was not unusual for me to arrive at the barn and find Wimpy out in the field with Tequila, lying between my horse's feet or stalking a squirrel in a nearby tree.

Paul was going back to Great Falls on business the next day, and offered to stop by Stoneridge and pick up Wimpy. He came to regret his offer. Wimpy, not knowing who this person was or where he was being taken, howled at the top of his considerable lungs during the entire hour's drive back to the farm. Paul pulled into the driveway. Wimpy heard my voice, and the howling ceased. As I got him out of his carrier, he wrapped his paws around my neck like he'd never let me go. He was my cat, and he was home; he never howled again.

Once we had him, however, we didn't know what to do with him. We took him down to the barn to let him see Tequila and Coco, but I was not going to leave him in a strange barn. Nor could we keep him in the house with the other cats: my female cat, Scooter, was deathly afraid of him; and my big male, Tigger, simply hated him. We fixed up a bed in the cellar by the water heater, and that is where he spent his nights for the next several months.

We also gave Wimpy a new name, or to be more

precise, he earned it. Paul kept his considerable gun collection in the cellar, and one night he left his best gun case open on the floor. Wimpy peed in it. From then on, we called him "Gunny," which actually suited him much better. A few months later, Tigger died, and Gunny was promoted to "upstairs cat." From that position, he ruled the house for the next five years. But upstairs or downstairs, it really didn't matter to Gunny. Like the rest of us, he was where he wanted to be.

After 23 years of living and working in the city, life on the farm was an adjustment. Life with Paul was an even bigger adjustment. Not only was it a matter of adapting my schedule to that of another person, but he came with 6 grown children and numerous grandchildren as well. From the beginning, they all wanted to meet this new woman in his life. Life was a constant stream of visitors, and two of the grandchildren became such frequent guests that they had a room of their own.

Settling into the new house was a joy. We took our time: we stained the barn a dark brown to match the new board fence. We ran water and electricity to the barn, and filled in and graded in front of the stalls where mud-holes used to be. I put in a vegetable garden, and hauled tons of rock to make borders for an array of flower gardens. Paul got to work finishing the basement, and soon we had a clean, dry recreation room and a library complete with overhead lights and pine paneling. We converted one section

of the basement into a tack room for me, with installed saddle racks and bridle holders and a huge
work table. Another part of the basement became
Paul's law office; a separate room became his tool-
gun-and-fishing room. Eventually, we even added a
swimming pool and an elaborate multi-leveled deck
connecting it to the house.

I loved having my own place, having total control over Tequila's schedule and being fully responsible for his care. It was a very special joy to wake
each morning and see him grazing contentedly right
outside my bedroom window. This was what I had
always dreamed of, and I felt truly blessed.

We developed a pattern: I took care of the day-
to-day work; Paul became the "special projects man."
I cleaned the stalls and mowed the fields, bought the
horse feed and the groceries, kept the house clean
and the gardens weeded. Paul repaired the gutters or
paneled the basement or constructed work-tables; it
was the kind of thing that fit in well with his schedule. While I wanted to stay home with the horses
after years of commuting and traveling, Paul was a
wanderer. He always seemed to be planning a trip
somewhere: a fishing trip with one of his boys; a ski
trip with a grandson; a deer-hunting expedition with
his Army buddies. He took one grandson to the Foot-
ball Hall of Fame and on a ski trip to the Cascades.
Another grandson got to go skiing in the Andes in
Chile. And there were frequent trips to the West Coast
to visit his mother and sister.

We joined a Catholic community at a nearby Army post, and became involved in church activities; it was something I had not done since my college days, and it was to prove a life-giving experience in more ways than one. Paul was admitted to the Virginia Bar, and donated many hours of his time to pro bono work for indigent defendants.

Then there came a day when Paul decided that he wanted a horse, too. It made sense: we had three stalls; three horses were as easy to care for as two; and, we reasoned, it would give Tequila a companion if anything happened to Coco. How could we possibly have known at the time that little Coco, who was then well into her forties, would outlive almost all of us!

We did what we always did in such cases: we asked around. It was my veterinarian who found the "perfect" horse for Paul. His name was O'Henry, and he was a semi-retired thoroughbred hunter who had had a hard life, and was facing a harder one if someone didn't rescue him. We looked at him: a lanky bay with a tangled mane and tail, and a perceptible lack of courage. I rode him. I liked him. We bought him. What is more, when we brought him home, Tequila liked him, too. O'Henry stayed.

Paul had owned a horse named Copper many years before. The horse was sold when Paul was sent to Vietnam, and he hadn't ridden since. He had a good sense of what to do, but I have to be honest:

my husband was not a good rider. He could stay on as long as the horse didn't do anything unusual – which translated into a pretty precarious seat, especially on O'Henry!

O'Henry was a nice enough horse, but he was terrified of his own shadow. He was afraid to cross the stream. He spooked at the sight of a piece of paper on the ground. He went crazy every afternoon when I took Tequila away on a trail ride, galloping up and down the fenceline whinnying frantically for his friend. Having Coco in the field with him made no difference at all; she was so small that he didn't consider her to be a horse.

O'Henry particularly hated big orange trucks – or machinery of any kind. Needless to say, Paul frequently took him up to the road: that was the way we got to most of our trails. And almost as frequently, Paul returned with a bump on his head or a cut on his leg, or even a bruised spleen where O'Henry had freaked and dumped him onto a fence or into a ditch. One day I watched in horror – and a modest amount of amusement – as Paul rode O'Henry the 30 feet from the barn to the start of a our own woodline – and O'Henry saw something he didn't like, wheeled frantically, and dumped Paul flat on his back. Parachute training was no preparation for being dropped from a height of 5 feet!

We had owned O'Henry for about two years when Paul was hospitalized for the second of four surgeries that he would undergo during our married life. This one was the most serious: to repair an abdominal aneurysm. Between hospitalization and recuperation, he was out of commission for several months. During that time I rode O'Henry almost every day, in addition to my daily rides on Tequila.

It was a mixed blessing. O'Henry never dumped me; in fact, he discovered that he didn't intimidate me at all. If he started to back up, I would firmly keep backing him until he tired, or back him into a pine tree or a fence. If he shied at a calf in the field, we would trot circles around that calf until he was thoroughly bored with it. I was trying to break him of his dangerous habits, but it was probably too late for that.

O'Henry was a very different horse from Tequila, mentally and physically. In retrospect, I was clearly too hard on him. I let him gallop when he was physically well past the age and condition when he could or should do such things. The second time we galloped, he popped a splint (broke the small bone in his left front leg), something that colts often do, but not horses in their twenties. The break caused no permanent damage; his leg was sore for a week or so and we did quiet trail walks. But I could not seem to get it through my head that O'Henry was not as tough as Tequila.

One day, after I had been riding him for a few months, we were trotting across a field that was still partly frozen. Some dogs were roughhousing in the vicinity, and they spooked O'Henry, who took off at a canter.

The ligaments in his front legs had been weakening for some time, a condition caused at least in part by his habit of "weaving," or swaying from side to side whenever he was in his stall. This time, I felt a sudden "give" in his right front leg, and he bobbled to a halt. I dismounted and walked him home. He was extremely lame, and his pastern, the rough equivalent of his ankle, was sinking with every step.

My veterinarian, Dr. Helen Poland, came in response to my call. She shook her head. "He's done major damage," was her immediate verdict. He had snapped the check ligament, which holds the entire support system in a horse's leg together. When it goes, the whole ligament structure goes, and there is nothing holding the leg together. Helen called a farrier specialist, Donnie Maley, who in time became my regular blacksmith and a good friend. Donnie constructed a special combination shoe and brace: the device looked like a metal cast and went halfway up O'Henry's leg; but still the internal support system continued to collapse.

We realized after a day or so that nothing more could be done. We had to put O'Henry down – on my husband's birthday. It was one of the worst days of my life.

Tequila did not miss O'Henry. With the exception of little Coco, he had never bonded with another horse. As long as he had his pony, and his "Mom," he was happy.

Just as we had at Stoneridge, we developed a comfortable daily riding routine. Most of the time I let Tequila choose our route. He preferred the vast open fields across the road from our farm. These fields also connected to a lovely wood with a stream running through it, and most days found us riding in that area. The neighbors began to look for us each day, standing in the window and waving as we passed by. To this day, one of the trails through the woods is known as "Lawrence Lane."

The fields were home to hundreds of cows, and many is the time, when no one was looking, that we would single out and chase a particularly active young steer who seemed to want to play. One summer we had a whole collection of favorites, known by their ear-tags as "Number 93," "Number 95," and "Number 97." As they bucked and bellowed and ran, with Tequila and me in hot pursuit, I think they enjoyed the game as much as we did.

Another favorite pastime in those fields came during haying season. The farmer would rake the hay into long windrows – and Tequila would start at the bottom of the field and jump them, one after the other. The farmer didn't mind our antics as long as we didn't disturb his handiwork. But he did shake his head in amusement one day, and commented as we rode up to the gate, "You must have got that horse for free. He's too wild to buy!" The day he saw me galloping Tequila bareback, he didn't stop talking about it for weeks.

On many of our rides we were accompanied by two neighborhood dogs: a white part-German shepherd named Speedy, and a wonderful curly-haired, terrier-type, scruffy little mutt named Rascal. They loved to run, they loved the companionship, and they enjoyed having a "purpose" to the outing. Besides, they never knew where we might go, and for them, too, it was always an adventure.

Rascal was by far my favorite canine companion. He was well named. He was quick, and full of fun. He had one ear that stood up and one that flopped over, and his curly white hair completely obscured his eyes. One of Rascal's favorite occupations was to catch onto a cow's tail with his teeth - and go for a ride! Sometimes the cow would take off at a run, in which case Rascal would skid behind. Other times the cow would swing its tail in great arcs, trying to dislodge this strange creature. At those times Rascal would happily fly through the air, legs and ears flapping as he was flung round and round. Rascal loved it.

The only time I ever disciplined Rascal was once on a trail ride when he made a major miscalculation. Tequila and I were galloping across the field – and Rascal tried to catch Tequila by the tail. The distraction could have caused Tequila to misstep. I could have been thrown. Rascal could have been kicked and killed. I halted my horse, swung out of the saddle, and beat the tar out of the little dog. I remounted, rode completely around the 100 acre pasture – and returned to find Rascal still cowering in the same spot, terrified to move. He never tried that again.

We had other routes as well: through the woods behind the house; across Black Horse Farm and through their thickets and fields; across Licking Run and up the gravel road to another farm with wonderful fields. But I have to agree with my horse: the farm across the road was the most fun.

Just beyond the cattle farm was another large estate, with its own landing strip. Usually the family flew in and out in their white Aviancas. But they also entertained a ballooning club, and many an early Saturday morning the horses and I were startled by the sight and the sound of balloons right overhead. Sometimes, when they were having trouble gaining altitude, they would be only 100 ft or so above my barn, pumping hydrogen into the great multi-colored globe, and calling back and forth, to each other, and sometimes to me. Tequila came to enjoy the sport, but some of the horses we had over the years never quite became accustomed to the sight.

As well-adjusted as he was, even Tequila could sometimes be triggered by something REALLY different. One such experience came one evening when we were riding in the cow pasture. We both heard a strange roaring, and then the sound of people laughing and talking, and the clinking of glasses. We looked up and saw, right over our heads, the Sea World Blimp, coming in for a landing on the airstrip. It was exciting for us to see them, and I imagine it was equally exciting for any of them who were looking down, to see a little palomino streaking ahead of them, racing them toward the woodline.

Life was very good on our farm. We were settled in; we had fixed it up the way we wanted it; the horses were never happier than in their own barn. I was thoroughly pleased with the blacksmith and with Helen, my veterinarian, a gentle, brilliant woman who became a close friend. She had her own practice, with other veterinarians working for her, but she usually chose to see Tequila herself. Only once did she send a staff member to administer routine shots; poor Scott, a newly-minted veterinarian, got to the barn before I did, and came flying out sputtering, "I hope I'm in the wrong place!" Tequila was simply standing in his stall, but he had drawn himself up to his full 14.3 hands, arched his neck, pawed and pranced, and the good doctor wanted nothing to do with something that intimidating.

Whether it was a matter of age or contentment, Tequila also stopped jumping fences. Only once after we moved to the farm did he jump a pasture fence. It was wintertime, and the grass in the two paddocks which were open was being eaten down. The back field, however, was growing lush, and I was trying to save it for springtime. Tequila had a different idea, and one morning I looked out the kitchen window to see him on the other side of the fence, down by the pond, sampling his springtime supply.

Actually, as he grew older and more arthritic, our jumping was of necessity curtailed. Even on a good day, it was not wise to stress his joints any more than necessary. We would pop over fallen logs or trees on the trail, or jump the little windrows, but as he reached his mid-twenties, that was pretty much the extent of it.

Much as I hated to admit it, Tequila was starting to slow down. But he would not have been Tequila if there was not an occasional exception, and like much of what Tequila did, one incident in particular was quite extraordinary. It was an early summer day, and we had taken an extra-long ride through the woods on the far side of the cattle farm. The trail wound for a couple of miles, and as we approached the fields again, we saw a fallen pine tree that had not been there a few weeks before. It blocked the trail, and the brush on both sides made it impossible to go around. What is more, under the tree was a yellow feed bag with the carcass of a dead calf inside, and two big dogs were gnawing at it vigorously. We had already been out for almost two hours, and we had two choices: go back the way we had come, or jump the tree.

Tequila and I stopped, and we talked it over. I looked at the scene before us, with the fallen tree and the snarling dogs, and told my little horse it was his decision. I turned him around and started trotting back down the trail toward the woods, but on a loose rein. He took the signal. Suddenly he spun, picked up a strong trot and then a canter – and sailed over the tree, the carcass, the feedbag and the dogs. It was a brilliant jump for any horse, but especially for a 28-year old!

As we shared the elation of a job well done, neither one of us could have known that it was also his last.

COME UNTO ME

*"Even though I walk through the valley of
the shadow of death, I fear no evil."*

Psalm 23

1993 marked the beginning of the crisis years of
my life. The word "crisis" means "a turning point,"
and my life indeed took a radical turn.

My first vivid memory of 1993 was a telephone
call from my younger sister, Sandy. She said she had
had a lump on her breast for several months, and it
wasn't going away. "Get to a doctor!" I said with as
much urgency as I could convey, all the while shaking
my head and wonder

ing what had taken her so long to speak of it. It
was one of many instances where I failed to
understand my sister.

Sandy was eight years younger than I, and
sometimes seemed like my polar opposite. Where I
had spent my childhood playing with blocks and
trains and exploring the woods and befriending
animals, Sandy wanted pretty dresses and dolls, and
spent long hours watching television. The differences
carried over into adulthood: while I followed a career
in academia and government, she went to work for a

cosmetics company in Hollywood, California. I was up to my neck in politics; she bragged that she had never voted. We hardly knew each other growing up, and saw little of each other as adults.

Sandy visited me three times during my years in Washington and Virginia; they were not happy occasions. After one visit, in fact, she composed a three-page written critique of all that had gone wrong on her trip: the time I spent with Tequila topped the list. Still, she was a beautiful girl with long brown hair and big blue eyes, a generous soul with a wicked sense of humor. Now, however, she was in trouble. And I wanted to help.

The tumor proved to be malignant, and was far advanced. She insisted that she didn't need my help: she had her husband, and our mother lived nearby. She would have the surgery, go through chemotherapy, and everything would be fine.

Everything was not fine. She finished both chemotherapy and radiation, and less than a month later a lump appeared in the other breast. There was a second mastectomy. This time, I flew to Colorado to be with her. I was shocked at what I found. Not only was my sister suffering greatly, but my mother, whom I had not seen in four years, was entering the advanced stages of Alzheimer's!

From a distance, Mother had hidden the condition well. She used pat phrases: "It's on the tip of my tongue." "It just slipped my mind." "I did it yesterday." Of course, there were clues: her letters sometimes made little sense, but I had attributed it to advancing age. Her gifts came wrapped in weird paper or contained inappropriate items, but again, I attributed it to her age. I was not prepared to find a woman who had always dressed like a fashion model, wearing a sweatshirt over a full skirt and eating dinner at 3 o'clock in the afternoon. I suspect the change had come on so slowly that my sister didn't notice at first. And by the time Mother's disease had progressed, Sandy was fully absorbed in her own deteriorating condition.

I learned from the apartment manager that Mother had inadvertently set fire to her kitchen. I learned from a neighbor that she often drove to the grocery store and could not find her way home. Mother had learned to drive after my father passed away in 1976, and she had already had four accidents in 15 years. I took her car keys away; if she missed them, she never said. I began looking for an assisted living facility that could take her on short notice; she could not continue to live on her own, and living with Sandy was out of the question at this point. I also began taking trash bags full of papers – letters, bills, stock statements, bank records, and reams of solicitations and Publisher's Clearing House mailings – back to my sister's house where I sorted through them at night.

Riding, which had always been a relief and a joy, became more important to me as I sought to escape from these pressing problems. Riding required my complete attention; I was fully absorbed in the moment. I savored the rhythm of Tequila's gait, the wordless communication from my mind and body to his. I loved the wind in my face as we flew across a field, the sense of oneness with another creature and with the beauty of the world around us.

Thus it came as a particular shock, one day in late July, when we cantered to the top of the cow pasture and he suddenly came up sharply lame. It was his right front foot again, and I assumed another abscess or stone bruise. I dismounted, checked his foot, loosened the girth and led him home.

A visit from Helen Poland produced the all-too-familiar diagnosis: "It's probably a stone bruise." It was certainly possible; the ground had baked to the texture of cement in the summer heat. But a stone bruise would have cleared up in a few days, and this didn't get any better. If anything, it got worse. Helen came back to the barn and took radiographs – and phoned in disbelief with the results. Tequila had foundered, badly. "He's rotated 18 degrees!" She was horrified. "We have to do something right away to keep the coffin bone from coming through the sole of his foot." "Keeping the bone from coming through his sole" was to become a major preoccupation for both of us for the next three years.

Tequila's condition was severe enough to warrant outside help. Helen placed an immediate call to Dr.

Ric Redden, a noted Kentucky veterinarian and farrier, who air-shipped a specially designed boot of his own devising. Its purpose was to take the pressure off the toe and the sole of the horse's foot by "de-rotating" the axis of the coffin bone. First the horse's heel had to be cut back as far as possible to realign the bone with the sole of the foot. Then the hoof was fitted with a hard plastic boot with hard rubber wedged inserts, which would prevent any further pull of the tendons supporting the coffin bone, and thus relieve pressure from that direction.

The treatment required that the horse be kept in his stall; the foot had to be kept quiet if it was to heal. But Helen knew all too well that would never work for Tequila, so I was allowed to handgraze him outside the barn twice a day, keeping his walking to an absolute minimum. The combination of the boot and the anti-inflammatory drugs which we were administering was supposed to stop the rotation. It did not.

As Tequila's right front coffin bone rotated to an alarming 25 degrees, Helen puzzled over the cause of the problem. It was then that I recalled his probable founder several years before, when he had the infection in his right front leg. Radiographs of his left front foot revealed that the coffin bone in that foot was rotated seven degrees. It was an old and stable rotation. Clearly, the problem had started years before, and the combination of age, wear, and the weakening effects of successive abscesses over the years, had finally brought it to a head.

However, we were now faced with an even more complex situation: a long-standing weakness offered a poorer prognosis. Still, Helen assured me that there was hope – as long as his coffin bone didn't "sink" as well. When a coffin bone sinks, it drops down from the ligaments that hold it in place, thus making the internal structure of the foot even more unstable.

In mid-September, a new radiograph showed that the bone had sunk. For a while, our hopes sank with it. Helen and I began to discuss the possibility of euthanasia; we reviewed Tequila's considerable tolerance for pain; we weighed his quality of life. Euthanasia was a decision I dreaded having to make. I was to learn, in time, it is not a decision to be made, but a course to be followed when nature dictates it.

Tequila, meanwhile, was handling the situation in his own way. Somehow, our treatment was keeping him relatively pain-free. He was eager to go out every day; he dragged me around the field as I held his leadline trying to contain him. He even broke loose a couple of times and trotted and cantered to his favorite grazing spots. Most of all, his attitude was great: he was bright, alert, trusting, affectionate, and accommodating of the treatment.

"How's everyone's favorite horse today?" became Helen's salutation as she called in regularly to check on her special "client." She never referred to Tequila as her "patient" – he was her one and only horse

CLIENT. She did not need an intermediary human owner to communicate with HIM.

Just as she had done before with O'Henry, Helen now called in Donnie Maley, a farrier who specialized in coping with difficult cases. Donnie was an artist and a craftsman, and he devised a unique backward shoe and pad arrangement which kept the weight off Tequila's toe and sole and put it back on the heel, which was more stable. It was a strange looking shoe. Instead of attaching to the hoof wall with nails like an ordinary horseshoe, this one was built with a "gooseneck" in front, and attached to the front wall of his hoof with two screws. Two regular nails held it to the heel.

An arrangement like that could not be left open to the elements: it would catch on the grass or a vine, and pull, or it could get packed with dirt. Every day I had to soak his foot in Epsom Salt, apply a poultice to the sole to toughen it, and wrap the entire shoe and hoof in packing and duct tape.

With the new shoe, however, there came a welcome degree of stability; and a new freedom for Tequila. The deterioration of his hoof was finally halted. In fact, in time we were able to reverse the rotation to only 15 degrees. Tequila could now be turned out by himself or with his pony in his pasture. His gait remained a little "off," but he could still do a credible trot and canter. Despite his infirmity, he was a happy horse.

Still, even as we watched him graze, we knew we were living on borrowed time. Helen was prompt to inform me that she had never had a horse founder this badly and still survive. Her response to nearly all my questions became, "I don't know. He'll have to tell US." We were in uncharted territory, and we were learning from him.

In the midst of my anxiety about Tequila, I also made several more trips to Colorado to help my mother and sister. The treatment program of chemotherapy, radiation, and eventually a bone marrow transplant, left Sandy increasingly debilitated – and depressed. There were many days when she could not even get out of bed.

I helped where I could. I drove her to her doctors' appointments. I did food shopping, fixed meals, and tried to keep up her spirits. Simultaneously, I was doing what I could for my mother, who by now failed to recognize my sister, her favorite daughter and her lifelong companion. Mother kept asking for "the other Sandy" – the Sandy who was well and happy and fun. Eventually, she settled for calling ME Sandy; if it eased her pain, it was fine with me.

During my travels, Paul was able to care for Tequila, to soak and wrap his foot, and to keep him safe. But Tequila missed me, and I missed him. I called home every night to get a full report. And because my favorite cat, Gunny, was also taking my absences very hard, Paul began putting him on the phone so he could hear my voice.

In June of 1994, I returned from a trip to Colorado to find that Gunny suddenly looked terrible. Gunny and I were very attached: he slept with his head on my shoulder every night, and he cried whenever I left him. I thought at first that he had just mourned my absence. But he was thin, and his eyes were hollow, so I made plans to take him to the vet for a checkup. Before I could do that, he died in his sleep, lying in the bedroom window in the afternoon sun. I picked up his little body, and held him, and cried. And for the first – and surprisingly, ONLY – time in my life, I asked the question, "How will I live the rest of my life without him?"

But life did not allow much time to think about that, or even to mourn. Sandy's condition was worsening, and in early September 1994, she passed away. We buried her in Estes Park, Colorado, and brought my mother back to Virginia to a nursing home. By this time, Mother had no idea where she was, or what was happening to her. She never knew about my sister's death. She arrived in Virginia with a virtually empty suitcase; the nursing home claimed it was "all she had." It took several months and a complaint to the State authorities to get the rest of her belongings released to me.

I began volunteering at Mother's new facility as a way of getting her involved in activities. I did a weekly "reading group," and helped with an exercise class. I was now balancing Tequila's care with almost daily visits to my Mother. And then Paul needed another surgery as well.

A typical day might well involve giving Tequila his medicines and handgrazing him for a couple hours in the morning, then driving to the nursing home in Manassas to visit with my mother and take her on a drive or an outing. I would then come home in time to take Paul to a doctor's appointment, and spend the afternoon handgrazing Tequila again before soaking his foot, rewrapping it, and putting him in for the night. In between, there was the house to care for, the barn to keep clean, the shopping to do, the lawn to mow – and the visitors kept coming! It is no wonder that the years 1993-1996 remain a blur in my mind.

To make matters even more complicated, I still wanted a horse I could ride. I dearly loved riding, the physical challenge of it, the intimacy with nature, the long hours on the trail away from the telephone and other distractions. While I knew I could never find another Tequila, I hoped I might at least find a horse that I could enjoy. I searched high and low, followed up on ads, drove from farm to farm trying out mounts. I rode horses that I had no business riding, and ended up riding one that no one should have ridden – he was too much of a rogue.

Helen tried to warn me that he wasn't "suitable." But he vetted sound, he was healthy, young and pretty, and I decided to take a chance. Ringing in my ears was a pronouncement many years ago by my friend Ben Franklin in Great Falls. He watched me ride Tequila one night and commented, "If you can ride that horse, you can ride any horse there is." Unfortunately, I believed him.

But trying to ride Crackerjack was an exercise in futility. I foolishly began taking him out on short trail rides alone. He was extremely difficult to control, but I thought it was just the newness of his surroundings; he would get better as he settled in, I told myself. And so I continued riding him, not only against the advice of my veterinarian, but also against the obvious advice of the one who had the best judgment of all – my own horse, Tequila. Tequila did not like Crackerjack, and I soon learned why.

I had been working with the horse for a few weeks, and was finishing a session in the field right next to the farm. I rode up to the gate, and started to dismount. With my left foot still in the stirrup and my body suspended over the middle of his back, Crackerjack swerved, bolted, and took off bucking and galloping. My first thought was, "I don't want to be dragged!" And so, I tried to remount. With all the bucking and twisting that was going on, getting back in the saddle was impossible. As I felt myself going off over his right side, I said a simple prayer: "Please God, not my back or my neck."

I landed on my back, and heard a crack. I lay there for a few minutes. I could move my arms and legs (though I could tell that my right hand was broken), and I could turn my head. Gingerly, I got to my feet, walked back to the barn, and sat on a bale of hay talking to Tequila who had watched the proceedings from his stall.

As the pain and the realization that I was really hurt began to settle in, I walked up to the house, asked Paul to get Crackerjack in, and then take me to the Emergency Room. X-rays confirmed the diagnosis: I had broken vertebrae in my back. For the first time in my life, I spent a night in the hospital. The next day my wonderful orthopedist came in, announced that if I could still walk I would be OK, and sent me home. The rib cage would act as a brace, he explained; I could walk all I wanted to. But I could not lift anything, and I definitely could not ride. At least I could soak Tequila's foot and groom and graze him and do his medicines. But the heavy work carrying water buckets, hoisting hay bales and cleaning stalls – fell on Paul for the next few weeks. Fortunately he was sufficiently recovered from his surgery to be able to handle the load.

I sent Crackerjack to a training facility, where they worked with him for a month and arranged for his sale.

I was not ready to give up, however, and some months later I bought a lovely horse named Brett. He was an Arab-Appaloosa cross with all-over "leopard" markings and a mane that stood straight up on end. I called him my "polka-dotted punk." He had good manners and a wonderful sense of humor. While they were never turned out together, Tequila nuzzled him through the stall bars and gave him a passing grade.

Brett was a horse I could play games with: he loved to sneak up behind me in the field and give me a butt with his nose, or take the hat off my head with his teeth and run around the field tossing it like a toy. Unfortunately, however, he was not confident going out on the trail by himself, and he started to see "gremlins" where none existed. The day that he spotted some frightening "creature" in the woods and took off across the field bucking was the day we came to a parting of the ways – literally.

Brett had a particularly nasty corkscrew buck, and the condition was probably exacerbated by the fact that my saddle was not a good fit for him. As I discovered later, the saddle had actually slipped over his withers during his antics, which probably accounted for the fact that I came off. But I was not happy as I lay in the grass just a few yards from where Crackerjack had dumped me only a few months before. And I was even less happy to make a return trip to the Emergency Room to make sure nothing else had been broken!

Brett had to go, and I am happy to say I found the perfect place for him: an equestrian bed and breakfast establishment in the northern part of the county, where he is now known as "Perfect Prince." He has the run of the place, and rules the barnyard.

My final attempt to find a riding horse was an old soul named Dusty. I knew nothing about his background; his last assignment had been working for a stable that offered hourly trail rides, and he had been used to carry prospective investors around a site that Disney hoped to turn into a theme park. Whatever he had done in life, he clearly had not enjoyed it. I bought him because he seemed safe, and because he needed a good home. He came with a bill of sale that read, "One aged gelding, as is." I thought I could make him happy again, but it was too late for that.

I rode Dusty for a few months. But he did not enjoy trail rides; he simply did not enjoy work. And if he didn't enjoy it, neither did I. I kept him as a companion horse for Tequila and Coco, and began making references, only partly in jest, to my "assisted living facility" for older horses.

Meanwhile, my mother's condition continued to deteriorate. Alzheimer's is a despicable disease. It robs the person of their very being. My mother had always been quick and lively, full of fun, very musical and talented with crafts. She lost it all: the ability to crochet, to play a piano, to tell stories, to understand jokes.

Communication with my mother on my level was impossible; I learned to communicate on hers. And while she could not appreciate the irony, it was the capabilities I had developed with Tequila which helped me to understand her.

Most communication with an animal is non-verbal. It is sign language, body language, inflection, eye contact; it is tactile, sensory, and psychic. We humans rely far too much on words, and we miss the more subtle signs that often are more nuanced than speech. I learned to sit with my mother, who would rattle on in words that made no sense, but I would follow her hands, her smile, the tone of her voice, the look in her eyes. And then, by sensing the mood she was conveying, I could pick out a single word or a hidden thought, ask a question about it, comment on it – and be rewarded with a dazzling smile: I had understood!

I think it was during these years that I reached a new plane in sensitivity to suffering, and also the ability to treat it with humor. My mother and I could laugh together over a silly word or the antics of a squirrel. My horse and I could enjoy a game of modified "tag" around the field. Suffering doesn't have to be somber; it can bring moments of joy.

Tequila lived for almost three years after his initial diagnosis. They were years of hope and heartbreak, of tension and tenderness, of keen observation and close participation with his health care professionals. They were times of learning for us all, and of a deepening of the understanding and the love that had sustained us through all our years together.

My veterinarian and farrier watched Tequila in

awe, amazement, and affection. *We* might know that there was a major problem, but *he* kept going strong. He nuzzled and teased little Coco; he cantered across his field; he pawed for his food – with his damaged hoof. Many was the time I would let him out to graze on the lawn as a special treat, only to find him an hour later half a mile away, up the lane or back in the woods. He developed a favorite route which took him through the adjoining property, into the woods, and back up the trail to his barn.

As we worked with him, Tequila taught us all some lessons which we hoped would help with other horses. We learned how to treat the most severe founder; how to keep him comfortable; how to adjust medications. Donnie devised new shoeing techniques, which he first tried on Tequila. Helen learned that a horse with will and courage could survive even the most adverse conditions.

Caring for Tequila was also a constant process of adjustment. I had to be able to limit his exercise to prevent damage to the foot or additional pull on the ligaments still attached to the coffin bone. I also had to be sure that he got enough exercise to keep him happy and otherwise healthy. His foot had to be protected from the elements: no dirt could get in and cause infection. Frozen or hard-baked ground could cause bruising of the sole; for those times, Donnie created a metal plate that screwed into the bottom of his shoe without touching the sole, thus absorbing all the hard contact.

We developed a routine. Tequila had X-rays done of his front feet every six weeks. I would lead him into the aisle of the barn and place his foot on a clean, smooth board. Using a hand-held machine, Helen would take the radiographs while I held the plates in place. She would then study the prints and meet Donnie at the barn a few days later to discuss the results. Together they would figure out just how much heel to take off, where to trim the sole, whether there were any possible pockets of infection. Once the X-rays showed a possible gas pocket developing inside the hoof, and they were able to drill through the hoof wall to relieve the pressure. Another time, there appeared to be a weakening of the side walls of the hoof, and such information guided the placement of the nails. All of us learned a lot in those three years, and Tequila was a willing patient and a unique teacher.

Caring for a horse in Tequila's condition is not something that can or should be undertaken by everyone. It requires an enormous commitment of time and resources. The hours spent handgrazing Tequila, soaking his foot, and administering medications numbered in the thousands. The cost of the numerous visits by the veterinarian and the farrier, the medications, the X-rays, the special shoes, the consultations with experts in the field, amounted to thousands of dollars per year.

I did it not just out of love, or a selfish desire to keep Tequila with me. I did it also because he had such a strong will to live, and I honored and respected that. I did it out of curiosity: where would the path take us? What might we learn that could help other horses in the future? And finally, I did it out of hope; I never gave up thinking that Tequila just might recover.

Of course, he never did. Rationally I knew Tequila was slowly declining. I could see it in my mother at the same time. I tried to give each of them my attention, my care, and my love.

I visited my mother almost every day while she was in my care. I was with her when she suffered a massive cerebral hemorrhage which was the beginning of the end. And when the end did come for Mother, in December 1995, I was by her bed, holding her hand, stroking her hair, and telling her I loved her. I flew her back to Houston to be buried next to my Dad.

The winter of 1996 was harsh, with cold winds and blizzards. Tequila thrived in it. He was out in the snow every day. He plowed through four foot drifts to find a patch of grass. He moved more comfortably in the snow that he had in years, because the snow provided a welcome cushion for his foot. He bucked and galloped like a foal on those frosty winter mornings.

But there is an inexorability about nature, and about deteriorations. While they may be slowed, they can never be halted. One morning in mid-March I arrived at the barn to find him "cast" in his stall; lying down with his legs pinned against the wall, unable to get up. I got a rope around his legs and flipped him over onto his good side, and helped him up. He ate his grain, and went about his daily routine. But there was a new wariness which we communicated to each other.

Tequila, always a sturdy horse, began to lose weight. A week later he was cast again, and this time I had a much harder time helping him to his feet. The spunk seemed to go out of him at that point, and he was very lame. This time the radiographs showed that the tip of the coffin bone had actually broken off. My faithful veterinarian, Helen, provided a trailer and we took him over to her surgery. It was a Sunday, and I assisted as she cleaned out the bone chips, smoothed off the tip of the bone, and opened up an abscess at the same time. Donnie came and participated in the operation, and constructed yet another remarkable shoe with a revised metal plate.

In the end, it was not the founder which brought him down, but a new complication: kidney failure. Tequila had been on medication for years, and since he had foundered his doses of anti-inflammatories and painkillers had necessarily been increased. But the medicine was taking a toll on his kidneys, and he began drinking – and eliminating – copious amounts of water. The medication was contributing to renal failure; but without the medication he could not survive the pain. This time Helen called the best HUMAN doctors she knew to get their medical advice. They all said the same thing: this was the end of the road.

Nature had made the decision for us. On April 18, 1996, Helen came to the barn early in the morning to give Tequila one last shot of a powerful painkiller. I handgrazed him on the lawn for hours, letting him enjoy as much of the rich spring grass as he wanted. I brushed him, carefully and lovingly. It was a lovely warm spring day, and the time together was a treasure.

Helen came back in the late afternoon with a man with a backhoe. He dug the grave in a spot I selected: I wanted Tequila to be buried on the farm, where he would be near. When the time came, I walked him to the spot and Helen administered the final, lethal dose. I held him in my arms as he breathed his last, his head once again in my lap. Then I stood up, and said, "He's still beautiful." He was, and is, and ever shall be, my beautiful Tequila.

We buried him where he lay, beside the garden.

REVELATION

"Give thanks to the Lord for He is good, his mercy endures forever."

Psalm 118

Every ending is also a beginning, though it took me a while to realize it. With the death of Tequila just four months after my mother's death, the hole in my life was now crater-sized. I had spent the past three years taking care of Tequila, my mother, my sister, and Paul, who had now had three surgeries in seven years. These tasks had taken most of my waking hours, and most of my energy, physically, emotionally, and mentally. Even as I grieved, I also pondered: What will I do now?

As Tequila was laid to rest, Helen and I tried to console each other. There was going to be a big hole in her life, too. Tequila had been her favorite, and certainly her most time-consuming patient, for many years.

After a while, I walked down to the barn. I still had Coco, and she deserved to be well cared for. In addition, there was Dusty, Tequila's companion horse, who now needed a companion horse of his own. I had to think of the living, while mourning the dead.

Once again, Helen came to the rescue. She found a lovely gray thoroughbred mare named Sleepytime Gal. Gal was a beauty, exceptionally well-bred, and with several Stakes wins to her credit. She was now in her mid-twenties and could no longer bear foals. Her owner was happy to give her to a good home. Dusty and Gal became wonderful friends, and we enjoyed her exquisite presence for the next two years.

For a time, things seemed to settle down. I wasn't riding, but the horses were happy, and my "equine assisted living facility," as I jokingly called it, was taking on the aspects of a permanent arrangement. I resumed volunteering in a real such facility, a nursing home in Warrenton, where I read stories to the elderly residents and visited them on a regular basis. I had learned from the time with my mother how much visits and outside contact are appreciated, and how few elderly residents ever get to enjoy them.

But life is not meant to stand still, and mine was not peaceful for long. One Sunday morning I went down to the barn to feed the horses and was shocked to fmd my beautiful mare rolling in agony in her stall. I got her up, walked her out on the grass, and shouted to Paul to call Dr. Poland. It was one of the few times that Helen was not available, and her associate came instead. We tried everything: pain killers, muscle relaxants, and purges. But Gal just kept getting weaker. Finally, by mid-afternoon, we had no choice but to put her down. How I wished that Helen had been there! Her associate, Dr. Tena Boyd, and I stood there totally puzzled, then agreed that we needed to know what had gone so terribly wrong. Was it something we had done, or failed to do? Together, we performed a necropsy, right there in the back yard. What we discovered was a massive tumor that had been growing around her intestine for years. There had not been a single indication of discomfort until that fateful morning, when it had finally cut off the blood supply. We knew then there was nothing we could have done.

Dusty was bereft without his friend, and I needed another companion horse for him immediately. Once again, I was fortunate. The Activities Director at the nursing home offered me a saucy little retired Tennessee Walking Horse named Rusty. "Rusty and Dusty" became the talk of the neighborhood, and they were delightful together: two little old chestnuts who grazed side by side.

It wasn't long before I discovered that there was a good reason why they were always together: Dusty was losing his sight! He had developed a condition called uveitis, a clouding of the retina, which if left untreated can ulcerate, and can also spread into the brain. Even with the best of treatment, it can eventually cause blindness.

Once again, Helen became a regular visitor to my barn. We tried ointments, antibiotics, all the recommended treatments. Dusty not only failed to respond, but the condition spread to his other eye.

This time Helen came up with an experimental approach, which left me convinced that she was really trying to recruit me for her practice: it involved treating Dusty's eyes with his own plasma. Every morning, I had to draw blood from his jugular vein, refrigerate the vial until the plasma separated, then draw the plasma into a small syringe and squirt it back into his eyes. It worked, at least well enough to retard the progression of the disease.

By this time I had given up all thought of riding. It is possible to ride a sightless horse, but only if there is a strong bond of trust between horse and rider. Dusty had come to me too late in his life for that trust to develop; he had had too many bad experiences with people along the way. In addition, I had been diagnosed with osteoporosis, and had been warned by my orthopedist that I could not sustain another fall. You can't ride if you can't afford to fall. I decided to quit while I could still walk and run!

To compensate for the loss, we put in a swimming pool. It was one of the best things I ever did. Every day – and sometimes two and three times a day – from the end of April til the beginning of October, I was in my pool, happily swimming laps while keeping an eye on my equine charges.

Then the unexpected struck once more, this time with a vengeance. In January of 1999, Paul had a fourth surgery, this time to repair a torn rotator cuff. It was slow to heal, and eight weeks later his shoulder still had not healed enough to permit him to drive. One day I was driving him home from a physical therapy session at the hospital. We were on a four-lane highway and within sight of the turn-off to our country road, when a car suddenly cut across the highway and slammed into us broadside. The driver, who was under-insured and sustained no injuries, was charged, innocuously with "failure to yield."

I have almost no memory of the accident. I was told that it took almost an hour to extricate us from the car, while a helicopter stood by to transport us to Inova Fairfax Hospital. Paul died in the helicopter. I spent the next week heavily sedated in the shock-trauma unit, with injuries that included broken ribs, a punctured lung, a broken collarbone, and something called a "crushed chest."

For the first and only time in my life, I received the "last rites" of the church, a sacrament now more appropriately referred to as the "anointing of the sick." Paul and I both served as members of the Board of our Catholic community, and the outpouring of support was beyond anything I had ever experienced or even dreamed of. My room was filled from morning til night with visitors bearing plants, flowers, cards and gifts. Our priest, and my good friend, Fr. Hank Lemoncelli, OMI, was a daily visitor and an incomparable source of support. With his help I was able to make the funeral arrangements from my hospital bed, choosing readings and hymns, designating pallbearers and musicians, deciding on a burial site at the Culpeper National Cemetery.

I received a tentative release from the hospital the day of Paul's funeral, with the understanding that I was to stay in a wheelchair, and to return if any problems developed. I did neither.

There was a blizzard the night before the funeral, and ten inches of snow covered the ground. A wonderful neighbor who was also a Fairfax County fireman drove through the blizzard, arriving at the hospital at 9 p.m., to bring me the clothes I had chosen to wear to the funeral. In view of the weather, I expected a small gathering, and was truly stunned to find that two other Oblate priests had joined Fr. Lemoncelli, the principle celebrant, including one priest who had driven all the way from Buffalo, New York! Among the 250 people in attendance, there were friends and relatives I hadn't seen in years; friends and associates of Paul's whom I had never even met; all six of Paul's children, and even his ex-wife!

After the funeral, and the burial with full military honors, and the luncheon back at the church, I was finally driven home. For the next several days, I entertained a seemingly non-stop parade of friends and family and well-wishers. It was a comforting distraction.

At first I could not even dress and bathe myself, and it was Paul's daughter-in-law, the mother of the two grandsons who had spent so much time at the farm, who now repaid the favor. For the first two weeks, she never left my side. When she did go home, my care was taken over by women from our church community, who brought home-cooked meals, cleaned the house, stayed with me at night, drove me to appointments.

It was a new experience for me, to be cared FOR, instead of caring for others. But far from being difficult to accept, I found joy in the care and companionship of friends. Maybe it was the example of Tequila, my lively and independent steed, who accepted his own infirmities with grace and equanimity. I learned that giving is an act of reciprocity, of mutual dependence and trust. Just as the giver finds joy in the giving, so the recipient, through grateful acceptance, gives back to the giver.

I pushed myself to walk a little farther each day; physical therapy was something I looked forward to. I opened the pool as early as possible that year, and swam twice a day. I gradually took over the care of the horses, and got back to gardening and mowing and other chores. By early summer, except for one noticeably dropped shoulder, I was as good as new.

I was also ready to reach out and do more. Partly it was a selfish motivation: I wanted the stimulation, the fun, of human contact. At least equally, I think, it was an expression of gratitude: I was still alive.

It was several months after the accident before I learned the full story of what had happened: it both frightened and inspired me. It had been a particularly horrendous accident; the car was crushed, and we were trapped inside. Most people who witness an event like that have absolutely no idea what to do, and are afraid to try for fear of doing something wrong.

In this case, the very first person on the scene was the most senior trained Emergency specialist from the Fairfax County Fire Department. Mike Runnels was, in fact, the one who trained the other fire personnel in advanced rescue techniques. He was driving a personal vehicle with no equipment on hand, but he borrowed a crowbar from a pickup truck driver, smashed open the rear window of my station wagon, and crawled inside. I was not breathing and was already turning blue. He repositioned me, summoned help on his cell phone, and called in the helicopter. He stayed in the car talking and trying to reassure us. When the local volunteer rescue squad arrived he directed them in safely extricating us. All the while, he thought that I was in the worst shape and would be the one to die. Paul's injuries were clearly extensive, but he was conversant throughout the ordeal. A ruptured aorta is not immediately visible.

Hearing this account several months later is an experience I will never forget. I knew then, in my heart of hearts, that my life had been saved for a reason. God had work for me to do, and I had better "listen up" and learn what it was.

I continued my volunteer work at the nursing home, and added to that a volunteer commitment at the hospital. I became one of the "escort volunteers," who staff the front desk, check people in, deliver papers and discharge patients. It put me in a position of greeting everyone who came in, and it turned out to be a wonderful way to keep track of old friends, and to make new ones.

My primary volunteer responsibility continued to be our church group. It isn't really a church, and it isn't really a parish: it is a Catholic community of people who support an order of missionaries, the Oblates of Mary Immaculate. The Oblates had served the Vint Hill Catholic Community for many years, under a contract with the Department of Defense. In 1997, Vint Hill was one of many military establishments closed as a budget measure. But our Catholic community wanted to stay together. Under the leadership of Fr. Lemoncelli, we formed an "Oblate Club of Virginia," and I was chosen, in absentia, to serve as an officer. As the group evolved, so did my role in it, and I found myself writing a monthly newsletter, planning the programs for our monthly meetings, conducting the meetings, and chairing the Board meetings as well. I had the time for it, it gave me pleasure to do it, and I served as the group's Chairman for almost eight years.

But much as I enjoyed my volunteer work, and caring for the farm and the horses, somewhere in the back of my mind was a growing awareness that something was missing. I found I was spending a lot of time alone – too much time, in fact. As I moved around the big farmhouse and cared for the barn and the fields, they somehow seemed empty. I started to see things that WEREN'T there, that had made the farm a real home: Tequila, Paul, and Gunny. I was becoming aware that much as I loved my life on the farm, it was taking up too much of my time. It was isolating me. The thought slowly began to dawn on me that maybe I should think of moving on.

The little pony Coco died in July of 1999; her aged body simply gave out. She was a plucky little pony to the end. As my veterinarian put it, at the age of 50, she had had TWO good lives, since the lifespan of a horse is generally considered to be 25 years. I buried Coco next to Tequila. They had been together in life for 20 years; they could be together forever.

But the loss of Coco further frayed my connection to the farm. Rusty and Dusty were pleasant to have around, but I felt no special bond with them, nor they with me. My volunteer work was fulfilling; I enjoyed having some time for friends. But I also had the feeling I could be doing more.

Once again, opportunity knocked, though I didn't recognize it as such at first. In October, Fr. Lemoncelli was transferred to Rome. At first I was devastated by the loss; then I began to think. I had never been to Rome. What better way to stretch my wings than to visit Rome in the year 2000, the Jubilee Year and the beginning of the new Millennium! Arrangements were made for me to stay at the Oblates' General House in Rome, and I flew over for the most remarkable Easter Week of my life.

It was an Epiphany. The music, the works of art, the grandeur of the great cathedrals, the thousands of years of history, the millions of the faithful pilgrims, all overwhelmed me. Even the sounds of a bustling city were music to my ears. It was a whirlwind week of churches and concerts, pasta and pictures, St. Peter's and the Coliseum. I returned home with my mind and heart overflowing with new images and hopes.

I walked in my kitchen door, looked around, and said to myself: "I don't want to live here any more."

The next day, I called a member of our church community who was also a realtor, and we put the farm on the market. Within a week, I had three contracts. Two months later, the farm was sold and I had bought a townhouse about midway between Warrenton and Washington. The townhouse was about half the size of the farmhouse, and of course there was no barn, or fields, or pool, or even much yard to care for. Huge chunks of my time were suddenly free!

Of course, I still had Rusty and Dusty. I found a farm about five miles from my new home where I could board them; the arrangement lasted about three months. First, Dusty contracted a terrible disease known as Equine Protozoal Myelitis, EPM. It is transmitted through contaminated hay or feed, and attacks the neurological system. Dusty started stumbling, then became partially paralyzed, then lost the ability to eat. Once again, Helen and I worked side by side, and once again, we had to put a horse down. It is never easy.

That left me with Rusty, who was adjusting well as a companion horse to a huge beast named Solid State, the retired fox-hunter who belonged to the owner of the barn where I was boarding. Then, less that two months after Dusty died, the owner of the farm died suddenly of a heart attack! At that point, I was left taking full care of Rusty, and of a horse I didn't even know. This certainly was not part of the plan; I did not want to be responsible for another farm! I called Rusty's former owners, who were only too happy to take him back. Life was telling me, in no uncertain terms, that my life with horses was over.

There I was, in October of 2000, without horses for the first time in 25 years. To my great surprise, it was an unexpected relief. I gave the rest of my tack and equipment to friends or to the Pony Club, and I began in earnest to follow other pursuits. Washington beckoned, and I began taking the commuter train into the city several times a month, visiting the art museums I had neglected for years, and catching up with old friends.

I took on a major writing task, helping my former employer, Senator Brooke, with his autobiography. The process of reliving the many Senate battles we had fought and the wonderful times we had as "family" proved both therapeutic and enlightening. I dove eagerly into research projects, and resurrected letters and reports long stashed away in boxes in my closet. As I worked, I thought often of the fact that if I still had the farm, I would not have time to spare for such a significant and meaningful project.

I took on more volunteer responsibilities, becoming a volunteer coordinator at the hospital. My role with the Oblates of Mary Immaculate also expanded, when I was asked to serve on a national committee to promote and expand lay affiliate organizations, like our Virginia Oblate Partners, to work in tandem with the missionary priests. In time, I became editor of the Order's first national newsletter for Oblate Associates. I was even invited to serve on the Board of the Pastoral Center at a nearby Benedictine Monastery.

My life appeared to be settled. And that, I have learned, is just when God reveals that He has other plans. After four years in the townhouse, I was once again feeling restless; it was time to move on. I began making plans to leave Virginia, and Washington, and all that I had known for almost 40 years. In November of 2004, I moved, with my three cats, to South Florida.

It was not something that I had planned with care;

it was no well thought-out decision that brought me to this new place. NONE of the major moves in my life have been "carefully planned." The very first decision of my adult life – to attend Boston University – came about because I felt sorry for the recruiter sitting all alone in my high school cafeteria on "College Day," and went over to him. When then Senator-Elect Edward Brooke offered me a position on his Washington staff, I raced back to BU, burst into the office of my major professor, and jumped up and down chanting, "I'm going to Washington!" The story of how I got Tequila is recounted earlier in this narrative; it was done with no thought at all. Even the decision to marry Paul was not really a decision, it just evolved from our relationship.

The move to Florida came about in the same way. One day, I simply knew I was doing it. None of these decisions, however, was haphazard, and I certainly have never regretted any of them. They can more accurately be described as opportunities that presented themselves, and I simply said "Yes."

Saying "Yes" to life is what this book is all about. I truly believe there has been a pattern in my life, that there were times when I was meant to say "Yes." And each "Yes" has added a chapter to a wonderfully full life. Now in the seventh decade of that life, I still greet each day as a gift, and a new adventure.

People often ask me: Do I miss horses? Sometimes. Do I miss riding? Yes. Do I miss Tequila?

Always in my life.

As I look back over my quarter century with horses, what I feel more than anything else is a limitless sense of gratitude. I am grateful, of course, for Tequila: for the experiences we shared, the challenges we faced together, the special love we knew. I am grateful for all that Tequila taught me: to live fully and laugh often, to love generously, and in the end, to grow old with grace.

I am grateful for all the worlds my horse opened up to me: for physical achievements I never thought were possible; for the beauty of nature which I never would have appreciated if I had not shared it with Tequila; for teaching me the true meaning of partnership, and love, and commitment, and ultimately, of faith.

I am grateful for the many friends I have met only because of my horse; for the multitude of things I have learned; for all the unexpected directions my life has taken.

Horses gave me a new life. Because I can look at the past with joy, I can look to the future with hope. For that, too, I am grateful.

God works in unexpected ways, and in my case, he worked through a horse. Tequila was not just any horse: he had the keenest love of life and adventure of any creature I have ever known. He taught me to be truly and always grateful for life's gifts, both great and small. He taught me to go where the spirit leads me, and always to give thanks. By giving this account of our life together, I give the gift to others, with all my gratitude.

I have always believed in guardian angels, those winged servants of God who carry us through the bad times – and the good. For twenty-one years, my guardian angel came, not with wings, but with flying hooves; not with a golden halo, but a golden mane; not with hands to guide me, but a heart to lead. Maybe horses are angels in disguise... .

EPILOGUE

One evening, on my second visit to Rome, Fr. Lemoncelli and I were walking in a small park near the Quirinale Palace, once the home of the Popes. I came upon a statue of a horse. It looked just like Tequila: the proud head, the arched neck, the taut, compact body. It was as if he had been transformed into bronze, and transported 5,000 miles away.

It was April 18, 2001, the fifth anniversary of Tequila's death. Through my tears, I took the sight as an omen, a signal that he was well.

I believe that God, who created us all, does not limit his love just to humans, any more than we limit our love just to our own species. God is love, and He clearly loves variety; and all that God loves becomes a part of his heavenly being.

I fully expect, if I arrive in heaven some day, that I will find a host of long-loved creatures arrayed there, waiting for me. Tequila will nicker, and Gunny will purr, and we will be whole again..

THINGS I LEARNED FROM MY HORSE

Start every day with enthusiasm – a good gallop clears the heart and mind for what lies ahead.

Explore each new path – you never know where it will lead.

Never pass up a chance to graze or drink –– you never know where the next treat may be coming from.

Be kind to others – especially those smaller than you.

Never try to jump a moving object.

Be curious about everything – some of it may taste good!

Don't let others set your limits.

Work through your pain – sometimes it goes away.

Don't fight back unless you have to – you can get hurt, too.

It's better to lead than to follow.

When you're in a race, do it to win – and have fun!

When you love, love with your whole heart – and love will be given back to you.

No matter where you roam – always come home at the end of the day.

Be in charge of your life – don't let anyone do anything to you that you don't want done!

Enjoy yourself – and others will enjoy you.

If you don't push the limits, you'll never know how far you can go.

And finally……..

Always give thanks.

Impact Christian Books

332 Leffingwell Ave., Suite 101
Kirkwood, MO 63122

AVAILABLE AT YOUR LOCAL BOOKSTORE, OR YOU MAY
ORDER DIRECTLY. Toll-Free, order-line only M/C, DISC,
or VISA 1-800-451-2708.

Visit our Website at *www.impactchristianbooks.com*

Write for *FREE* Catalog.